# Barrier-free Exterior Design:

CURB CUT

5' MIN.

4' MIN.

TRAFFIC ISLAND

PAINTED CROSSWALK MARKINGS

BOLLARDS

DRAINAGE GRATE

CROSSING LIGHT

WARNING STRIP

## anyone can go anywhere

Edited by GARY O. ROBINETTE, A.S.L.A.

Illustrations by RICHARD K. DEE, F.A.S.L.A. and CHRISTOPHER NOTHSTINE, A.S.L.A.

VNR VAN NOSTRAND REINHOLD COMPANY
New York

Printed in the United States of America

Published by Van Nostrand Reinhold Company Inc.
115 Fifth Avenue
New York, New York 10003

Van Nostrand Reinhold Company Limited
Molly Millars Lane
Wokingham, Berkshire RG11 2PY, England

Van Nostrand Reinhold
480 La Trobe Street
Melbourne, Victoria 3000, Australia

Macmillan of Canada
Division of Canada Publishing Corporation
164 Commander Boulevard
Agincourt, Ontario M1S 3C7, Canada

16 15 14 13 12 11 10 9 8 7 6 5 4 3 2

**Library of Congress Cataloging in Publication Data**

Robinette, Gary O.
    Barrier-free exterior design.

    Bibliography: p. 121
    1. Architecture and the physically handicapped.
I. Title.
NA2545.P5R58    1985    720'.42    84-27066
ISBN 0-442-22349-8

# Table of Contents

# Preface

This book is an outgrowth of the research which was undertaken to produce BARRIER FREE SITE DESIGN and the 3 volume series ACCESS TO THE ENVIRONMENT. This data gathering and the publication of those books was supported by the Department of Housing and Urban Development and by the Architectural and Transportation Barriers Compliance Board.

This is an expansion, an amplification and an updating of what was done a decade ago. In the early 1970's there was a need for sensitivity and for guidelines. There is now a need to show what has been done, how it was actually done and all of the ways it could be done.

There are a great many ways to plan, design and implement to insure unlimited access for all. Some ways of removing site barriers are more attractive than others, some are more effective and some are less expensive. It is possible to design initially to allow total access or it is possible to redesign or retrofit design solutions to specific situations. Initially every area had to be redesigned and retrofitted. Now many new and innovative solutions show how imaginatively any project can be designed to allow total accessibility.

Much has been done in the past two decades to remove barriers and to provide equal access to all facilities by all of the people in our society. Federal government agencies such as the Department of Housing and Urban Development, the Department of Education, the General Services Administration, the Department of Health and Human Services, the Department of Transportation, the National Park Service and the Architectural and Transportation Barriers Compliance Board, to mention only a few, have committed large sums of money and significant manpower to produce reports, give guidance and guarantee access. State and local agencies have extended the work into their facilities and jurisdictions through revised and strengthened legislation. Associations worked with their membership to monitor, guide and assist in implementation. A National Center for a Barrier Free Environment was formed to initiate and coordinate activities taking place throughout the United States. Individual designers have worked with clients and interested citizens on individual projects. A mountain of publications, reports and studies have been prepared and disseminated. Even the United Nations has focused international attention on the issue with a special year designated to deal with the problem.

Possibly most importantly after a great deal of money, time and effort was expended the American National Standards Institute revised and refined the ANSI Standard 117.1 which outlined the methods of barrier free design in all facilities.

This book does not and could not possibly cover in a comprehensive way all that has been or is being done. It is an updating and an expansion of what has been done earlier. What has been omitted from the earlier books resulting from this same research is now available in many other sources in much greater detail. Certain information which was available in a condensed form in those earlier studies is not contained in this book. Data concerning:

> populations or numbers of disabled persons,
> current legislation,
> organizations involved in barrier free activities,
> a definitive bibliography,

have been deleted. In place of that material, a good deal more drawings, sketches and examples have been included. The effort to insure that ANYONE CAN GO ANYWHERE is never ending, this is one more effort to make that possible.

# Introduction

Convenient access to the outdoor environment is frequently denied to many people in our society because of the manner in which outdoor elements are designed and constructed. Every person can expect to be physically handicapped either temporarily or permanently at some time during their lifetime. A mother pushing a baby carriage, a shopper whose arms are loaded down with packages, a child pulling a wagon, a pregnant woman may all find themselves unable to cope with a flight of stairs, a curb, or a door because of the design of these elements.

These people may expect to be relieved of their handicaps within a fairly short length of time. Unfortunately, there are also those who, through a permanent handicap, will always be inhibited in their movements.

The total number of permanently disabled people is growing dramatically. The primary reasons for this are better medical treatment and care, and as a direct result of this, increased longevity. With people living well into their seventies, eighties and nineties, it may be expected that the opportunity for a traumatic injury or a debilitating disease during their lifetime is greatly increased. Also, the wars that have occurred in our recent history have created large numbers of disabled persons.

In the past, the basic attitutde of the general population toward those with various disabilities was "Out of sight - out of mind." Current attitudes place more emphasis upon encouraging disabled people to lead more productive lives and to avail themselves of educational and employment opportunities. Coincidently with this, a national effort has been made to employ greater numbers of handicapped person in more diverse positions and locations. This, of course, requires that those with disabilities must be able to go easily to a place of education and employment. However, while barrier-free architecture, at least in public buildings, is becoming reality through federal, state and local codes and legislation, provisions to assure barrier-free site design have for the most part been neglected. This inadequacy has not been as intentional as much as it has been accidental.

Architects, developers and public officials can make all buildings free of barriers in the design and construction. But, if people can't get from building to building or from cars or buses to the buildings, then the total environment is not barrier free. The freedom and lifestyle of some will be curtailed at some time because of the way an area is conceived and constructed. This book deals with the areas between and outside those individual buildings. It is based on the assumption that, in time, all public and many private buildings will be without impediments or barriers. Then, if the components and part of our outdoor environment are carefully and sensitively enough designed, no one is "locked out" or inhibited in their physical access to any area or activity and, then, in effect ANYONE CAN GO ANYWHERE.

The following is a listing of the definitions of terms used in this publication.

## Definition of Terms

For the purpose of this study, it has been necessary to define particular handicaps, impairments, and restrictive devices so that they may be related to individual design elements. The terminology used below, with the exception of "temporary impairments," is generally accepted and used in literature dealing with the handicapped.

1. **TEMPORARY IMPAIRMENTS**
   **Temporary impairment** refers to any and all situations in which people become temporar-

ily restricted in their movements either through a disease or trauma that requires time to heal, or simply in performing the normal functions of everyday life. The pregnant woman, the shopper with his arms loaded with packages, the skier with a broken leg, and the woman wearing high heel shoes are all "handicapped to a degree" in their movements, but the duration of their impairment is relatively short-lived.

## 2. ACTIVITY IMPAIRMENTS
The term **activity impairment** generally refers to any sort of limitation which curtails the normal activities of a person. Most often diseases of the heart, lungs, or forms of arthritis and rheumatism are involved. Visual, audial or mobility curtailment are not included. In general, people with activity impairments cannot play strenuous games or engage in unlimited physical activity.

## 3. MOBILITY IMPAIRMENTS (MOBILITY "A")
A **mobility impairment** curtails the ability of movement or ambulation. It may be caused by such things as partial paralysis which has **not** been compensated for by the use of ambulatory aids, or the absence of extremities which have **not** been replaced by mechanical aids. Disabilities, deformities, or handicaps which curtail the movement of the person are included in this category.

## 4. MECHANICAL AIDS (MOBILITY "B")
### a. Wheelchair
A wheelchair is a chair on wheels normally propelled by the occupant by means of handrims attached to the two side wheels. Wheelchairs may also be motorized or propelled by an attendant.

### b. Crutch
A crutch is a staff with a crosspiece at the top to support the person in walking. The point of support may be under the shoulder, upper arm, or forearm. For each crutch, a second support is provided at hand level.

### c. Cane
A cane or walking stick is a short staff either straight or curved at the upper end, used to provide some support at hand level in walking.

### d. Walker
A walker is a four-legged stand which provides support for the user. It is moved by lifting or by wheeling on casters.

### e. Brace
A brace is defined as any kind of supportive device for the arms, hands, legs, feet, back, neck, or head, exclusive of temporary casts, slings, bandages, trusses, belts, or crutches.

### f. Artificial Limb
An artificial limb is a device to replace a missing leg, arm, hand, or foot. It does not necessarily have moving parts. A device employed only for lengthening a leg where the whole leg or foot is present is not included in this definition.

### g. Special Shoes
Footwear specifically designed as podiatric aids to be used in assisting people in walking.

## 5. MANUAL IMPAIRMENTS
### a.
A **partial manual impairment** entails the impairment of either both hands to a certain degree, or total disability of one hand. It may refer to the lack of a replacement of a missing hand or arm with a mechanical device. There is some use of hands or arms, and some manual dexterity in a partial manual impairment.

### b.
A **total manual impairment** means, in effect, that the person has no use of his hands or arms. Therefore, he is handicapped in those aspects of the exterior environment which require the use of these extremities. It may be the result of arthritis, rheumatism, amputation, or the lack of replacement of a limb by artificial devices.

## 6. VISUAL IMPAIRMENTS
### a.
**Partial visual impairments** are usually caused by dysfunctions such as color blindness, the loss of partial sight in one eye, cataracts, glaucoma, a detached retina, or congenital birth defects. A worsen-

ing of some of these problems may cause
total visual impairments.

**b.** A **total visual impairment** means that a person has total loss of vision.

7. **AUDIAL IMPAIRMENTS**
   **a. Partial audial impairments** include people
   with a limited ability to hear, but who are
   still able to detect major sounds such as
   loud noises or audial warnings in the exteri-
   or environment.

   **b.** A person with **total audial impairment** cannot hear any sounds at all. Congenital birth
   defects, disease, or a steady audial deter-
   ioration which culminates in total deafness
   in old age are the usual causes.

8. **MENTAL RETARDATION**
   Mental retardation is defined today as a sub-
   average intellectual functioning which origi-
   nates during the developmental period and is
   associated with impairments in adaptive behavior. In less technical terms, the mentally
   retarded person is one who, from childhood,
   experiences unusual difficulties in learning
   and is relatively ineffective in applying what-
   ever he has learned to the problems of ordinary
   living. Degrees of mental retardation (mild,
   moderate, severe, profound) are measured by
   considering both measured intelligence and
   impairment in adaptive behavior.

# Basic Human Considerations

## People in the Environment

Unfortunately, too many of the public spaces in our nation have been designed based on criteria appropriate only to the non-handicapped portion of our population. Far from being a true representation of the human norm, our people, instead, are represented by a changing series of sizes, and requirements determined by both fate and specific circumstances of the moment. Years before, all adults were children, less than three feet tall, completely unable to accomplish many of the functions that are easily performed in later years. Even if a healthy person is fortunate enough to reach his elderly years without contracting a disabling disease or suffering a traumatic injury, he will most certainly experience the physical limitations brought about by the natural degeneration of his body. During the years the person is considered to be in their "prime", there is a continual occurrence of situations in which they are "handicapped" performing common everyday functions. Trying to open a door with an armload of groceries, moving an over-stuffed chair through a doorway, or trying to navigate a flight of stairs with a baby stroller are typical situations in which we all begin to understand, for a moment, the frustration which those with permanent disabilities face their entire life.

This report, therefore, is intended to present specific dimensional requirements and recommendations for designing our exterior spaces, both public and private, so that they might be completely accessible and usable by our whole population. It should be pointed out, however, that the data contained herein, has been gathered and condensed from a myriad of reports by others. While the dimensions have been determined by methods other than our own anatomical research, the information presented is felt to be a worthwhile contribution to this subject if it can serve to collect and synthesize the varying and sometimes contradictory recommendations published by the wide number of sources we referenced in gathering the raw material for this report. We have, therefore, selected those specific dimensions which in our opinion best represent the collective average of the recommendations of the many publications we reviewed. Accordingly they should be received with the understanding that the dimensions should not be viewed as finite or absolute but rather, as general guidelines which represent a sort of current "state of the art" among those publishing recommendations for the handicapped at the time of this writing.

## General Space Restrictions

In most instances designing a space that will accommodate wheelchairs insures that it will also be large enough not to be restrictive for other people using it. However, it should be borne in mind that spaces designed to allow for wheelchairs may be awkwardly large for certain semi-ambulant disabled persons who depend on narrow doorways, railings, and hallways for support. However, for practical reasons, the space restrictions shown here reflect basic wheelchair criteria.

1. **Wheelchair Dimension:**
    a. For design purposes, there are basically two types of wheelchairs differentiated mainly by the use to which they are put. They shall be referred to as small and large chairs.

       1. **Small Chairs:**
          The most commonly used wheelchair is the self-propelled model with the drive wheels either at the back or the front. The model with the drive wheels located at the back of the chair is very useful to people with strong upper limbs. This chair is superior in maneuverability compared to the front-wheel driven chair. Its center of gravity allows it to be piloted down steps, and up and down curbs, although it takes a powerful individual to perform such operations. It should be noted that attendants who push chairs prefer a rear-wheel driven model since, due to its better balance, it

# Dimensions for People Outdoors

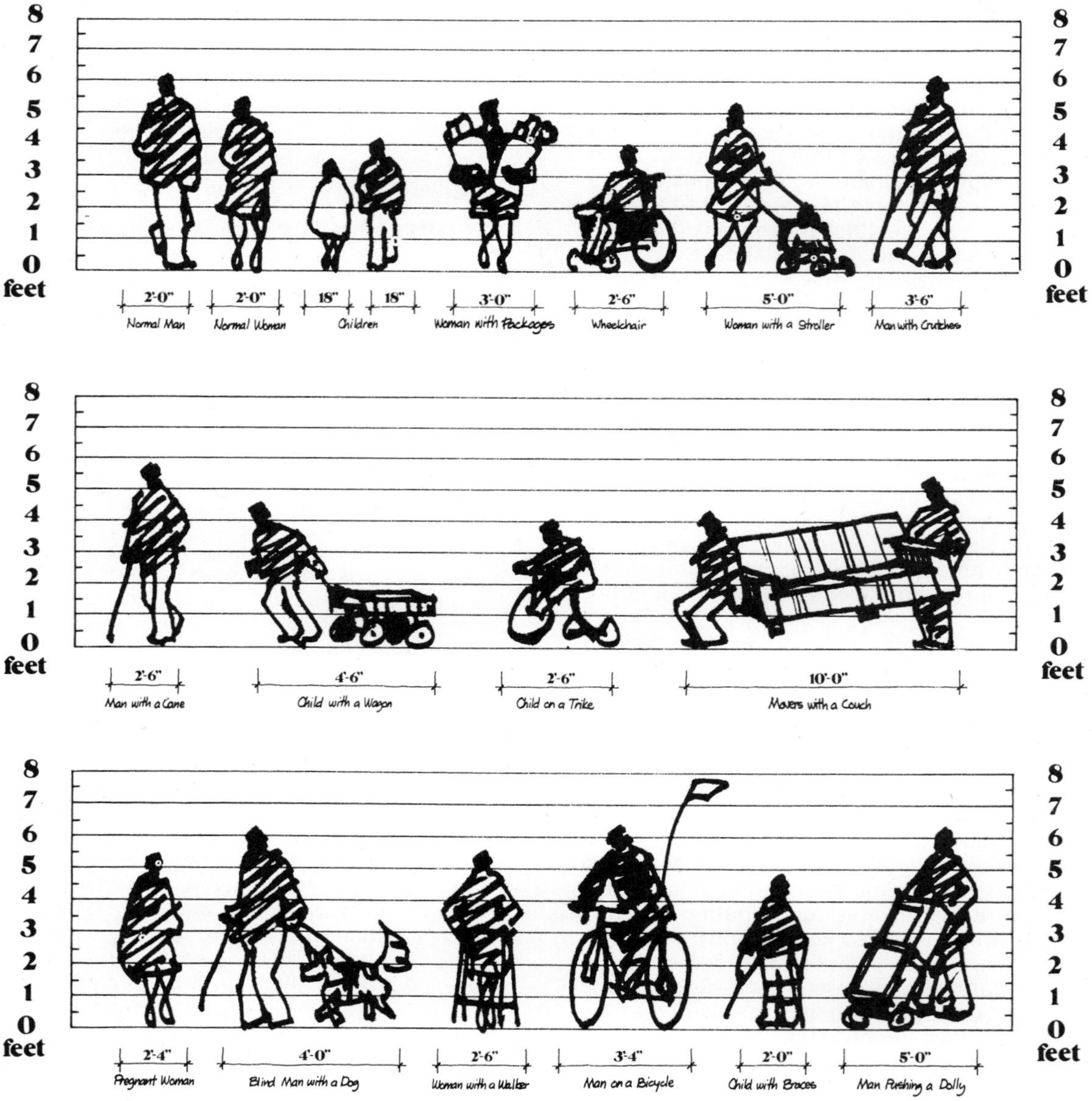
8
7
6
5
4
3
2
1
0
feet
2'-0"
Normal Man
2'-0"
Normal Woman
18"
18"
Children
3'-0"
Woman with Packages
2'-6"
Wheelchair
5'-0"
Woman with a Stroller
3'-6"
Man with Crutches
2'-6"
Man with a Cane
4'-6"
Child with a Wagon
2'-6"
Child on a Trike
10'-0"
Movers with a Couch
2'-4"
Pregnant Woman
4'-0"
Blind Man with a Dog
2'-6"
Woman with a Walker
3'-4"
Man on a Bicycle
2'-0"
Child with Braces
5'-0"
Man Pushing a Dolly

is much easier to push up over obstacles such as curbs or stairs than the front-wheel propelled model.

The front-wheel driven model is easier to operate for people who are weak in the arms, but it is extremely difficult to use in climbing obstacles such as curbs. These chairs are especially useful in homes where their shorter effective turning radius and wider front wheels make them both more maneuverable and less resistant to carpeting than rear-wheel driven chairs.

### 2. Large Chairs:
These wheelchairs are primarily used by people who are unable to propel a small chair. They are, as the name implies, larger in respect to length, height and width, and lack the large drive wheels of the smaller chairs.

### b. General Dimensions:
General dimensions are given for both small and large chairs. Since so many different models exist, the sizes shown at right are representative of the larger chairs of the two groups.

### c. Straight Line Travel:
The minimum space requirements for straight line travel for both large and small chairs are shown at left. These dimensions are for both enclosed and open walkways.

### d. Turning Radii:
1. Small chairs with rear propelling wheels can spin on a center axis for a full 360 degrees in a circular space 5'-4" in diameter. Although front propelled wheelchairs require somewhat less space in which to turn, their use in the exterior environment is so limited that they need not be considered for design purposes.
2. Large chairs are not able to execute the same type of spin maneuver as is possible with small chairs. To make a 180 degree turn, a three point turn is necessary. The minimum of space to accomplish this forms a rectangle approximately 8'-0" by 7'-0".

### e. 90 Degree Turns from Straight-Line Travel:
1. Small chairs require a minimum space width of 3'-0" from which to turn into a space 32" wide.
2. Large chairs require a space width of 5'-0" from which to turn into a space 32" wide.

### f. 90 Degree Turns Through Doors Or Openings:
1. For small chairs, passage through an opening in a wall 32" wide requires that there be no obstacles within 3'-0" of the opening. As the opening width increases, the minimum obstacle distance lessens. (See chart at right)
2. For large chairs, access through doors or openings in walls 32" wide requires that there be no obstacles within 4'-3". As with small chairs, the obstacle may be somewhat closer to the opening as the door width increases.

### g. Doors or Gates Occurring At The Ends Of Narrow Passages:
1. The prime design criteria here is the small chair since it is important that independent chairbound persons be able to reach and operate gates or doors without restriction.
2. There should be a minimum of 1'-3" of space (preferably 2'-0") between the opening edge of a gate or door and nearest perpendicular restriction.

### h. Miscellaneous Design Situations:
In addition to the most commonly used dimensions previously mentioned, infinite design situations exist that may be restrictive to people either pushing or riding in wheelchairs, or to people pushing other wheeled devices such as strollers or dollies. A number of situations have been diagrammed to increase the designer's awareness of the many restrictive space combinations that comprehensive design solutions must accommodate.

# Dimensions & Turning Requirements

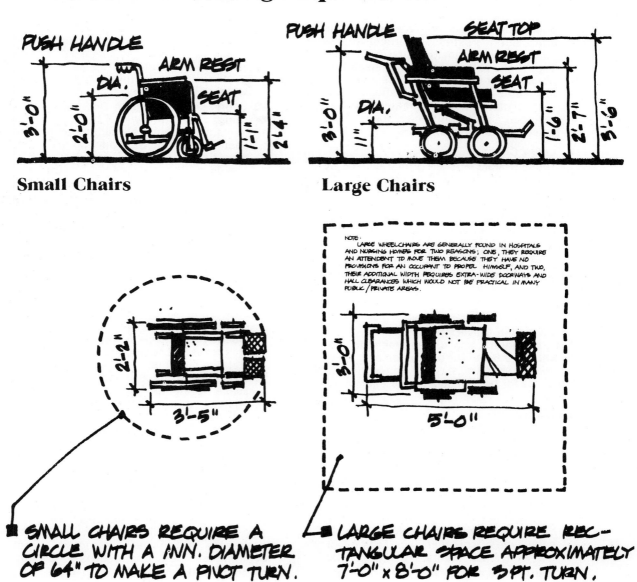

**Small Chairs**

**Large Chairs**

NOTE:
LARGE WHEELCHAIRS ARE GENERALLY FOUND IN HOSPITALS AND NURSING HOMES FOR TWO REASONS; ONE, THEY REQUIRE AN ATTENDENT TO MOVE THEM BECAUSE THEY HAVE NO PROVISIONS FOR AN OCCUPANT TO PROPEL HIMSELF, AND TWO, THEIR ADDITIONAL WIDTH REQUIRES EXTRA-WIDE DOORWAYS AND HALL CLEARANCES WHICH WOULD NOT BE PRACTICAL IN MANY PUBLIC/PRIVATE AREAS.

SMALL CHAIRS REQUIRE A CIRCLE WITH A MIN. DIAMETER OF 64" TO MAKE A PIVOT TURN.

LARGE CHAIRS REQUIRE RECTANGULAR SPACE APPROXIMATELY 7'-0" X 8'-0" FOR 3 PT. TURN.

# Dimensions for Wheelchair·Bound People

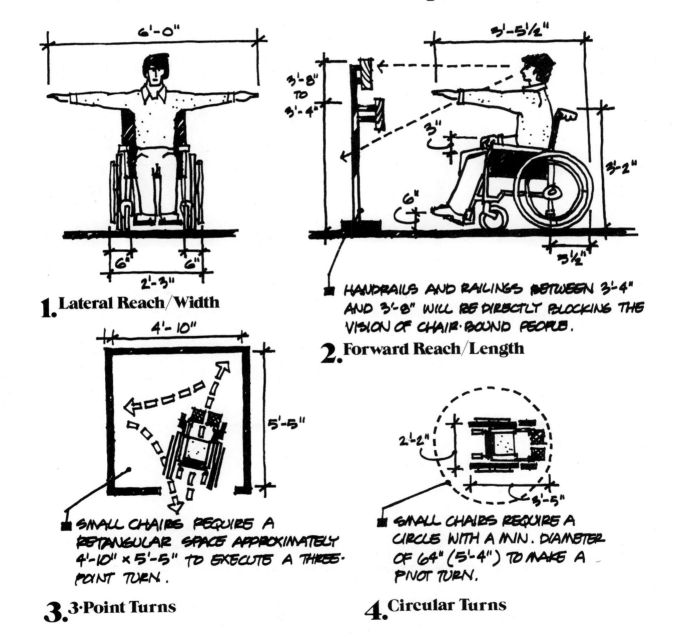

6'-0"

6"    6"

2'-3"

**1.** Lateral Reach/Width

3'-5½"

3'-8"
TO
3'-4"

3"

6"

3'-2"

5½"

■ HANDRAILS AND RAILINGS BETWEEN 3'-4" AND 3'-8" WILL BE DIRECTLY BLOCKING THE VISION OF CHAIR·BOUND PEOPLE.

**2.** Forward Reach/Length

4'-10"

5'-5"

■ SMALL CHAIRS REQUIRE A RETANGULAR SPACE APPROXIMATELY 4'-10" × 5'-5" TO EXECUTE A THREE·POINT TURN.

**3.** 3·Point Turns

2'-2"

3'-5"

■ SMALL CHAIRS REQUIRE A CIRCLE WITH A MIN. DIAMETER OF 64" (5'-4") TO MAKE A PIVOT TURN.

**4.** Circular Turns

# Recommended Widths for Straight-Line Travel

4'-0"

RECOMMENDED ONE-WAY

6'-0"

RECOMMENDED TWO-WAY

# Average Reach Limits for Adults in Wheelchairs

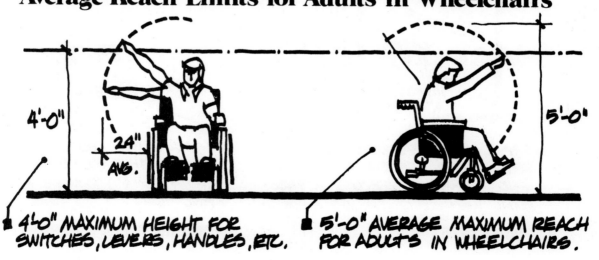

4'-0"

24" AVG.

5'-0"

4'-0" MAXIMUM HEIGHT FOR SWITCHES, LEVERS, HANDLES, ETC.

5'-0" AVERAGE MAXIMUM REACH FOR ADULTS IN WHEELCHAIRS.

# Dimensions for a Normal Human Figure

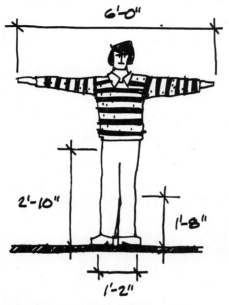

**1.** Standing, Lateral Reach

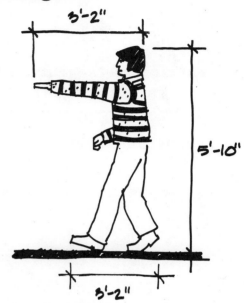

**2.** Walking, Forward Reach

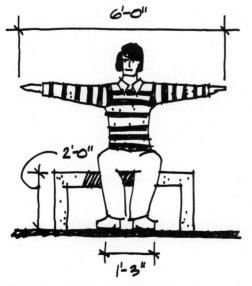

**3.** Sitting, Lateral Reach

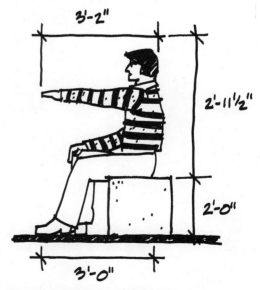

**4.** Sitting, Forward Reach

# Crutches, Braces, and Lower Amputees

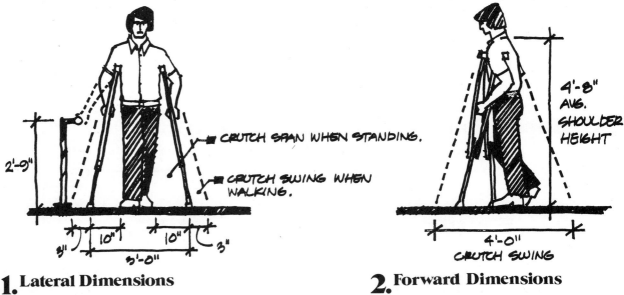

CRUTCH SPAN WHEN STANDING.

CRUTCH SWING WHEN WALKING.

2'-9"

3" | 10" | 10" | 3"

3'-0"

**1.** Lateral Dimensions

4'-8" AVG. SHOULDER HEIGHT

4'-0" CRUTCH SWING

**2.** Forward Dimensions

# Dimensional Requirements for the Blind

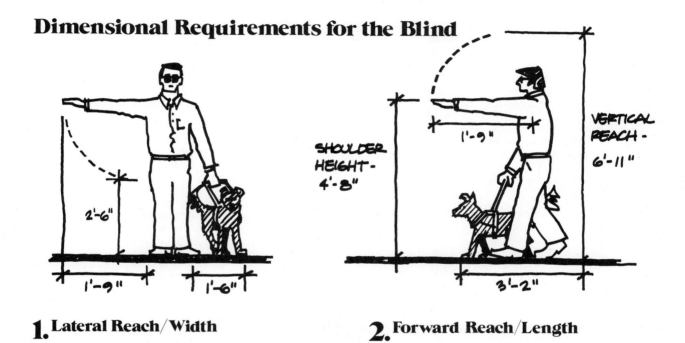

**1.** Lateral Reach/Width

2'-6"

1'-9"  1'-6"

SHOULDER HEIGHT- 4'-8"

1'-9"

VERTICAL REACH- 6'-11"

3'-2"

**2.** Forward Reach/Length

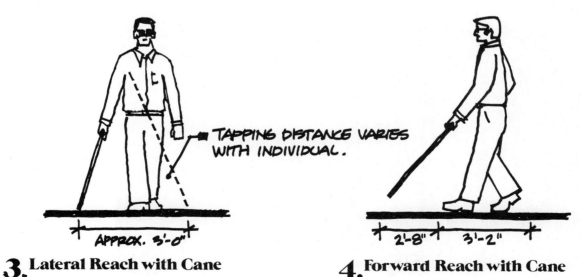

TAPPING DISTANCE VARIES WITH INDIVIDUAL.

APPROX. 3'-0"

**3.** Lateral Reach with Cane

2'-8"  3'-2"

**4.** Forward Reach with Cane

15

# General Site Accessibility

## Relating Site Components

Barrier-free site design is not some simplistic goal that can be achieved through the thoughtful handling of one or two problem areas on a site. The accessibility of any public or private outdoor area hinges on the physical relationships between design elements both inside and outside of the space. Unless there is a relationship of continuous accessibility between forms of transportation, site elements, and building entries, the value in making any one of these components more accessible is lost. Consequently, it is imperative that **all** elements of circulation be made as easily accessible as possible.

The following items should be considered to insure a good interface between transportation, site, and building entry elements.

1. Special transportation facilities should be provided for people who are restricted in their use of the exterior environment. Care should be taken to separate varying types of transportation where practical, since their point of intersection is usually confusing, dangerous, and delaying. Vehicular traffic should be separated as much as possible from bicycle traffic, and both should be held apart from pedestrian traffic.

2. In general, access to transportation facilities, through the site, and to buildings should be smooth and free of barriers which may prove impossible for physically restricted people to negotiate. Paving surfaces should be hard and relatively smooth, curbs should have ramped cuts, walks should be sufficiently wide to accommodate two-way traffic, and entrance walks to buildings should slope gently to the platform before the doors. If situations are present in which stairs are normally required, then at least one major entrance should be served by a ramp as well.

3. Doors into public buildings should preferably be activated by automatic opening devices. When these items are prohibited by costs, horizontal levers or through bars should be

installed on the doors.

4. Public conveniences such as restroom facilities, drinking fountains, telephones, elevators, and waiting areas, should be well organized and located in close proximity to building entrances. This allows people with physical limitations to gain access to necessary facilities with a minimal amount of hardship or embarrassment.

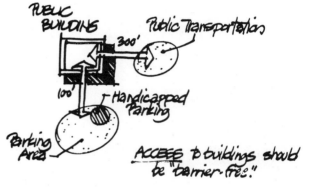

ACCESS to buildings should be "barrier-free."

# Doorways & Entrances

PUBLIC LOBBIES SHOULD CONTAIN THE FOLLOWING ITEMS IN AREAS ACCESSIBLE TO THE HANDICAPPED AS CLOSE TO DOORMATS AS POSSIBLE *:

- PUBLIC TELEPHONES
- REST ROOM FACILITIES
- DRINKING FOUNTAINS
- WAITING AREA WITH APPROPRIATE SEATING
- INFORMATION AND DIRECTIONAL SIGNAGE
- ELEVATORS, ESCALATORS, ETC.

* NOTE: ALL FACILITIES SHOULD BE FUNCTIONALLY USEABLE BY HANDICAPPED INDIVIDUALS.

## Doorways at Entrances

- MIN. 32" CLEAR OPENING.
- NO GRADE CHANGE AT THRESHOLD.
- HORIZONTAL THROW-BARS ARE RECOMMENDED OVER KNOBS, LATCHES, VERTICAL HANDLES, ETC.
- RECOMMENDED FORCE REQUIRED TO OPEN IS 5 lbs. TO 8 lbs.
- PROVIDE 18" SET BACK FROM NEAREST OBSTACLE (WALL, EDGE OF PAVEMENT, ETC.) SEE "GATES & DOORWAYS."
- PROVIDE AUTOMATIC DOOR AT HEAVILY USED LOCATIONS.

- ENTRANCE PLAZAS REQUIRE 10'-0" LENGTH FROM DOORWAY TO CHANGE IN GRADE (STAIRS)
- PROVIDE 5'-0" MIN. CLEAR SURFACE AT ALL LANDINGS FOR BOTH STAIRS AND RAMPS.
- RAMPS: MAX. % SLOPE = 8.33 %
  MAX. LENGTH/RAMP = 30'-0"
  MIN. ONE-WAY WIDTH = 3'-0"
  MIN. TWO-WAY WIDTH = 6'-0"
- PROVIDE ADEQUATE RAILINGS, HANDLES, CURBS, AT ALL STAIR AND RAMP LOCATIONS. SEE "STAIRS, RAMPS, AND HANDRAILS."
- PROVIDE SIGNAGE SHOWING POINTS OF ACCESS FOR HANDICAPPED PEOPLE.

AUTOMATIC DOOR TRUNDLE

RAMP

- PROVIDE 5 FOOTCANDLES LIGHTING AT ALL ENTRANCES.
- OVERHEAD CANOPY PROTECTS PEDESTRIANS DURING INCLEMENT WEATHER.
- MAX. GRADE CHANGE BETWEEN STAIRWAY LANDINGS = 6'-0"
- SEE "RAMPS, STAIRS, AND HANDRAILS" FOR DETAILS OF TREADS AND RISERS.
- PROVIDE MIN. 5 FOOTCANDLES OF ALL WALKWAYS, RAMPS, STAIRWAYS, SEE "LIGHTING CONSIDERATIONS."

**DROP-OFF ZONES:**
LOCATED AS CLOSE TO BUILDING ENTRY AS POSSIBLE; NO GRADE CHANGE BETWEEN ROAD SURFACE AND ADJACENT WALKWAY. DIRECT VEHICULAR CONNECTIONS BETWEEN DROP-OFF, SITE ENTRANCE, AND PARKING AREAS; SIGNAGE SHOULD BE PROVIDED TO DIRECT BOTH VEHICLES AND PEDESTRIANS TO DESTINATIONS ON THE SITE.

**BUILDING ENTRY:**
CLEARLY IDENTIFIED; ALTERNATIVE MEANS OF ENTRY PROVIDED FOR HANDICAPPED INDIVIDUALS (I.E. BOTH RAMPS AND STAIRS); PUBLIC FACILITIES LOCATED IMMEDIATELY OFF OF ENTRY IN LOBBY (LAVATORIES, PHONES, DRINKING FOUNTAINS, ETC.); NO GRADE CHANGES BETWEEN ENTRANCE AND FACILITIES.

**PARKING**
RELATED DIRECTLY TO BUILDINGS WHICH THEY SERVE; 'HANDICAPPED' STALLS NO MORE THAN 100' FROM BUILDING ENTRY.

**SITE ENTRANCE:**
WELL IDENTIFIED; OBVIOUS RELATIONSHIP TO BUILDING AND SITE IT SERVES; SIGNAGE TO DIRECT VEHICULAR AND PEDESTRIAN TRAFFIC TO DESTINATIONS ON THE SITE.

**WALKWAYS:**
SHOULD PROVIDE CLEAR, DIRECT ROUTE THROUGHOUT SITE; SURFACES SHOULD BE FIRM AND LEVEL; CURB CUTS AND RAMPS PROVIDED WHERE NECESSARY.

**REST AREAS:**
PROVIDED WHERE PEDESTRIANS MUST WALK LONG DISTANCES; KEEP REST AREAS OFF WALKWAY THOROUGHFARES.

**WAITING AREAS:**
PREFERABLY LOCATED WITHIN 300' OF BUILDING ENTRY; AREA LOCATED BETWEEN ROADWAY AND SIDEWALK TO AVOID TRAFFIC CONGESTION; AN OVERHEAD SHELTER IS RECOMMENDED FOR PROTECTION FROM WEATHER; ADEQUATE SEATING AND LIGHTING SHOULD ALSO BE PROVIDED.

**SIGNAGE:**
SHOULD BE PROVIDED TO DIRECT PEDESTRIANS TO VARIOUS DESTINATIONS OR AREAS OF THE SITE.

# Handicap / Site Element Relationship

## Site Elements

## Phys. Limitation

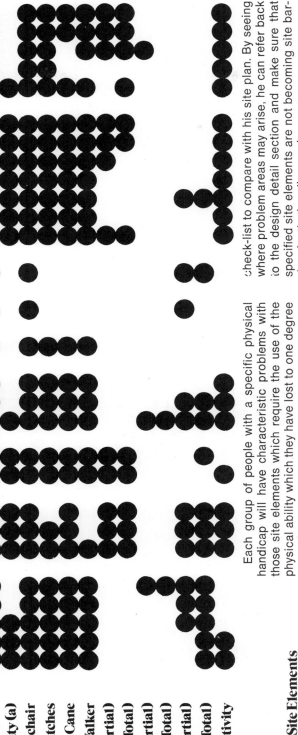

**Physical Limitation** (rows): Temporary; Mobility (a) — Wheelchair, Crutches, Cane, Walker [Mobility (b)]; Manual (Partial); Manual (Total); Audio (Partial); Audio (Total); Visual (Partial); Visual (Total); Activity

**Site Elements** (columns): Paving Surfaces, Natural Surfaces, Curbs, Drainage Grates, Intersections; Ramps, Stairs, Handrails; Gates, Railings; Waiting Areas, Drop-off Zones, Parking Areas; Plantings; Lighting; Signage; Playgrounds, Camping, Picnicking, Interpretive Trails, Spectator Areas, Fishing, Boating, Swimming; Seating, Tables, Public Telephones, Drinking Fountains, Trash Receptacles

Each group of people with a specific physical handicap will have characteristic problems with those site elements which require the use of the physical ability which they have lost to one degree or another.

These problems can be categorized in chart form according to the type of handicaps or limitations displayed and the number of site elements which will be placed on a site.

A chart like the one above gives the site designer or project administrator a quick-reference check-list to compare with his site plan. By seeing where problem areas may arise, he can refer back to the design detail section and make sure that specified site elements are not becoming site barriers for the handicapped.

To keep from being redundent, the definitions for the physical limitations have not been reprinted here. They can be found on pages 4 and 5. Likewise, the site elements can be found among the design detail sections.

**Site Elements**

**Physical Limitations**

Black Dots represent areas where site elements may cause physical barriers for handicapped people if the situation is not given special design consideration.

19

# Gate/Doorway Clearances

NOTE: All dimensions for both gateways and doorways.

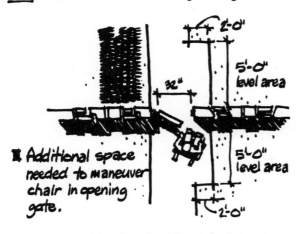

2'-0"

5'-0" level area

32"

5'-0" level area

2'-0"

※ Additional space needed to maneuver chair in opening gate.

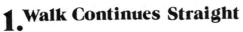

**1. Walk Continues Straight**

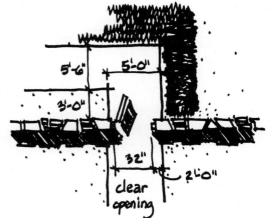

5'-6"      5'-0"

3'-0"

32"

clear opening

2'-0"

**2. Walk Turns With Gate Swing**

5'-0"

32"

2'-0"      clear opening

**3. Walk Turns Opposite Gate Swing**

3'-6"

2'-0"      32"

clear opening

**4. Walk Turns/Gate Swings Away**

20

# Ramp Landings and Doorways

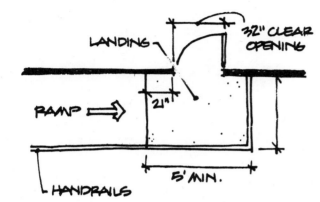

LANDING
32" CLEAR OPENING
RAMP
21"
5' MIN.
HANDRAILS

■ LANDINGS SHOULD EXTEND A MIN. OF 5' IN THE DIRECTION OF THE RAMP.

## 1. Side Approach

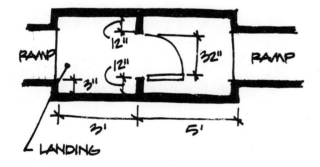

RAMP
12"
12"
32"
RAMP
3"
3'
5'
LANDING

■ WHEN RAMPS APPROACH A DOOR OPENING, ADDITIONAL SPACE MUST BE PROVIDED TO ALLOW FOR THE AREA COVERED BY THE SWING OF THE DOOR.

## 2. Direct Approach

32"
12"
12"
3'
5'
LANDING

■ DOORS SWINGING ONTO LANDINGS WILL REQUIRE ADDITIONAL CLEAR SPACE AT OPENINGS: 2' MIN. RECOMMENDED.

## 3. Swinging Doors

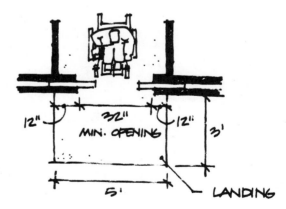

12"
32" MIN. OPENING
12"
3'
5'
LANDING

■ SLIDING DOORS REQUIRE NO ADDITIONAL LANDING SPACE.

## 4. Sliding Doors

# Doorway Considerations

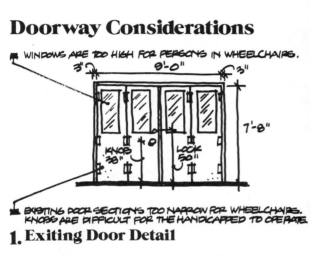

- WINDOWS ARE TOO HIGH FOR PERSONS IN WHEELCHAIRS.

3" · 9'-0" · 3" · 7'-8"

KNOB 38" · LOCK 50"

- EXISTING DOOR SECTIONS TOO NARROW FOR WHEELCHAIRS. KNOBS ARE DIFFICULT FOR THE HANDICAPPED TO OPERATE.

## 1. Exiting Door Detail

- THROW BARS ARE MORE EASILY OPERATED THAN KNOBS BY MOST HANDICAPPED PERSONS.

- ENLARGED WINDOW IMPROVES VISION FOR PERSONS IN WHEELCHAIRS.

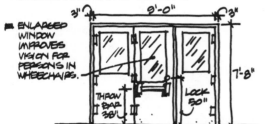

3" · 9'-0" · 3" · 7'-8"

THROW BAR 38" · LOCK 50"

- EXISTING 27" PANELS REMOVED AND REPLACED BY 36" SECTIONS, ALLOWING WHEELCHAIR ACCESS.

## 2. Proposed Door Detail

- NEW DOORWAY ALLOWS WHEELCHAIR ACCESS.

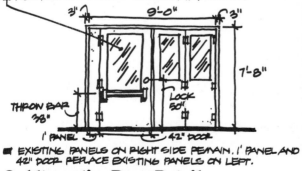

3" · 9'-0" · 3" · 7'-8"

THROW BAR 38" · LOCK 50"

1' PANEL · 42" DOOR

- EXISTING PANELS ON RIGHT SIDE REMAIN. 1' PANEL AND 42" DOOR REPLACE EXISTING PANELS ON LEFT.

## 3. Alternative Door Detail

Top photo: Entrances to buildings housing or frequently used by handicapped or disabled persons may be modified to provide grab bars or rails from the door to a driveway, all under a covered canopy.

Bottom photo: A courtyard in a classroom building at St. Andrews Presbyterian College in Laurinburg, N.C. was designed as a training area to help handicapped students learn to cope with common environmental situations.

Top photo: In order to help blind residents leave and come back to a multi-family residential unit, a continuous railing was provided from the entrance of the building to a nearby street.

Bottom photo: A covered canopy, a continuous grab rail and the removal of curbs or steps all help make this building entrance fully accessible.

# Walks and Intersections

## General Dimensions

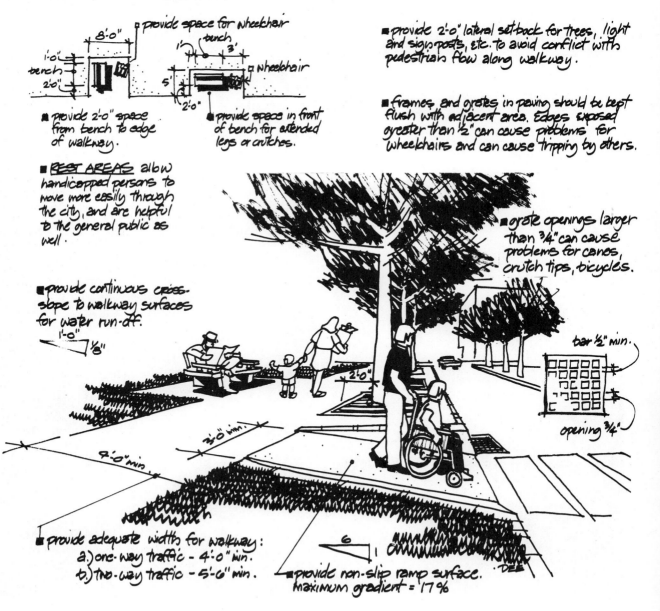

- provide space for wheelchair bench
- bench
- wheelchair

■ provide 2'-0" space from bench to edge of walkway.

■ provide space in front of bench for extended legs or crutches.

■ REST AREAS allow handicapped persons to move more easily through the city, and are helpful to the general public as well.

■ provide 2'-0" lateral setback for trees, light and sign posts, etc. to avoid conflict with pedestrian flow along walkway.

■ frames and grates in paving should be kept flush with adjacent area. Edges exposed greater than ½" can cause problems for wheelchairs and can cause tripping by others.

■ grate openings larger than ¾" can cause problems for canes, crutch tips, bicycles.

■ provide continuous cross-slope to walkway surfaces for water run-off.

bar ½" min.

opening ¾"

■ provide adequate width for walkway:
 a.) one-way traffic - 4'-0" min.
 b.) two-way traffic - 5'-6" min.

■ provide non-slip ramp surface. maximum gradient = 17%

# Walks

Walks should be designed to allow the greatest diversity of people to move safely, independently, and unhindered through the exterior environment.

Items to consider in the design or modification of walk systems are:

1. **Surfaces**
The surface or walks should possess stability and firmness, be relatively smooth in texture, and have a non-slip surface. The use of expansion and contraction joints should be minimized, and their size should be as small as possible, preferably under 1/2" in width. (The chart at the right shows some different types and characteristics of materials when used as walkway surfaces).

2. **Rest Areas:**
Occasional rest areas off the traveled path are enjoyable and helpful for all pedestrians, and especially for those with handicaps that make walking long distances exhausting.

3. **Gradients:**
Pedestrian paths with gradients under 5% are considered walks. Walks with gradients in excess of 5% are considered ramps and have special design requirements. (Also see "Ramps") Routes with gradients up to 5% can be negotiated independently by the average wheelchair user, but sustained grades of 4% and 5% should have short (5'-0") level areas approximately every 100'-0" to allow a chairbound person using the walk to stop and rest. Gradients up to 3% are preferable where their use is practical.

4. **Lighting:**
Lighting along walkways should vary from ½ to 5 ft. candles, depending on the intensity of pedestrian use, hazards present, and relative need for personal safety. (see "lighting considerations.")

5. **Maintenance**
Proper maintenance of walks is imperative. Where they are deteriorating, repairs should be made to eliminate any conditions that may cause injury.

6. **Curb Ramps:**
Changes in grade from street to sidewalk and from sidewalk to building entrances create most problems for people with physical handicaps. To facilitate movement over low barriers, a curb ramp should be installed. Surfaces should be non-slip, but not currugated as the grooves may fill with water, freeze, and cause the ramp to become slippery.

7. **Drainage Structures:**
Improperly designed, constructed, or installed drainage structures may be hazardous to people who must move over them. They should be placed flush with the surface on which they occur and grates having narrow parallel bars or patterns with openings larger than 3/4" should not be used. Grates should likewise be kept clean so as not to lessen the efficiency of the overall storm system. Obviously, a surface build-up of water, especially in the winter, may present a hazard. For this reason, drainage structures should not be located between a curb ramp and the corner of a street or immediately downgrade from a curb ramp.

8. **Dimensions:**
Walkway widths vary according to the amount and type of traffic using them. Walks should be a minimum of 4'-0" wide, with 5'-6" (6'-0" preferred) being the minimum width for moderate 2-way traffic.

9. **Wheel Stops:**
Wheel Stops are necessary where wheeled vehicles may roll into a hazardous area. They should be 2" to 3" high, 6" wide, and should have breaks in them every 5'-0" to 10'-0" to allow for water drainage off of the walk.

# Curbing

Curbing is a commonly specified element on most sites, and is in turn one of the most neglected items in regard to the physical barriers it creates. The problem is twofold; stemming from the attitude of most designers that 6"

# Surfaces for Walkways

## Comments

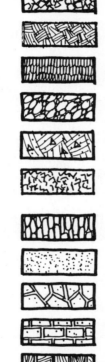

**Soft** (bracket grouping:)
- crushed rock
- earth
- lawn-grass
- river rock
- soil cement
- tanbark

**Variable** (bracket grouping:)
- cobble stones
- exposed aggregate
- flagstones
- sand-laid brick
- wood deck
- wood disks in sand

**Hard** (bracket grouping:)
- asphalt
- concrete
- tile/brick in concrete

### Soft Surface Characteristics

- IRREGULAR AND SOFT SURFACES MAKE WALKING EXTREMELY DIFFICULT FOR PEOPLE WITH MOBILITY HANDICAPS.
- POOR SURFACES FOR WHEELCHAIRS AND OTHER SMALL-WHEELED VEHICLES.
- THE BLIND HAVE DIFFICULTY WITH ORIENTATION.
- SURFACES ARE SUSCEPTIBLE TO EROSION.
- SURFACES WILL WITHSTAND ONLY LIGHT TRAFFIC.
- SURFACES ARE USEFUL FOR AREAS WHERE LIGHT PEDESTRIAN TRAFFIC WILL NEED A MODERATELY FIRM SURFACE, I.E. RECREATION AREAS, PARKS, NATURE AREAS, ETC.
- HIGH MAINTENANCE REQUIREMENTS, LOW INSTALLATION COSTS.

### Variable Surface Characteristics

- IRREGULAR SURFACES AND WIDE JOINTS MAKE WALKING EXTREMELY DIFFICULT FOR PEOPLE WITH MOBILITY HANDICAPS.
- JOINTS EASILY TRAP CRUTCH AND CANE TIPS, HEELS, NARROW WHEELS; JOINTS SHOULD BE FILLED AND NO WIDER THAN ½".
- IRREGULAR SURFACES MAKE MOVEMENT DIFFICULT FOR WHEELCHAIRS AND OTHER SMALL-WHEELED VEHICLES.
- ICE AND SNOW CAN BE A PROBLEM BY DAMAGING THE SURFACE OR BEING DIFFICULT TO REMOVE.
- MODERATE MAINTENANCE REQUIREMENTS, MODERATE TO HIGH INSTALLATION COSTS.

### Hard Surface Characteristics

- FIRM AND REGULAR SURFACES FOR WALKING AND MOVING WHEELED VEHICLES.
- JOINTS ARE KEPT TO A MINIMUM, LESS THAN ½" WIDE AND FILLED.
- ICE AND SNOW REMOVAL POSSIBLE WITHOUT EXTENSIVE DAMAGE TO SURFACES.
- HIGH INSTALLATION COSTS, LOWEST MAINTENANCE COSTS.

# Rest Areas Along Walkways

■ WHERE HANDICAPPED INDIVIDUALS ARE FORCED TO WALK LONG DISTANCES OR ENCOUNTER STEEP GRADES, (+5%), REST AREAS SHOULD BE PROVIDED.

■ PROVIDE MIN. 24" SETBACK IN FRONT OF BENCHES TO KEEP LEGS AND PACKAGES OFF WALK.

■ PROVIDE MIN. 36" SETBACK FOR WHEELCHAIRS.

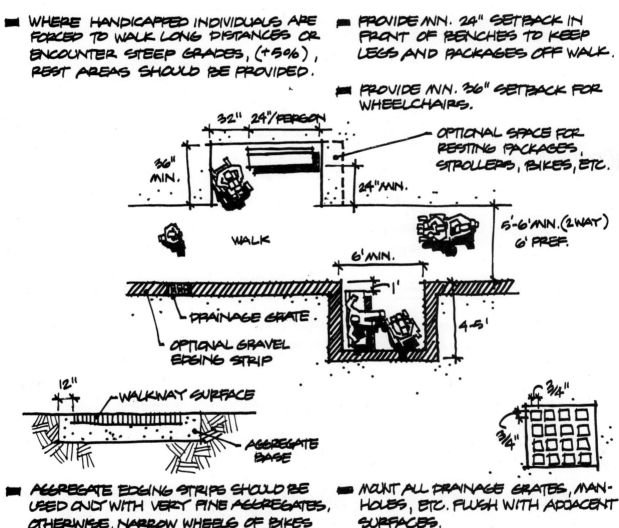

OPTIONAL SPACE FOR RESTING PACKAGES, STROLLERS, BIKES, ETC.

32" 24"/PERSON

36" MIN.

24" MIN.

WALK

5'-6' MIN. (2 WAY)
6' PREF.

6' MIN.

1'

DRAINAGE GRATE

OPTIONAL GRAVEL EDGING STRIP

4'-5'

12"

WALKWAY SURFACE

AGGREGATE BASE

3/4"

3/4"

■ AGGREGATE EDGING STRIPS SHOULD BE USED ONLY WITH VERY FINE AGGREGATES, OTHERWISE, NARROW WHEELS OF BIKES AND WHEELCHAIRS WILL PLOW DOWN INTO SHOULDER, POSSIBLY SPILLING RIDER.

■ MOUNT ALL DRAINAGE GRATES, MAN-HOLES, ETC. FLUSH WITH ADJACENT SURFACES.

■ GRATE OPENINGS SHOULD BE 3/4" SQUARE OR LESS.

## 1. Gravel Edges/Shoulders

## 2. Drainage Grates

# Walkway Considerations

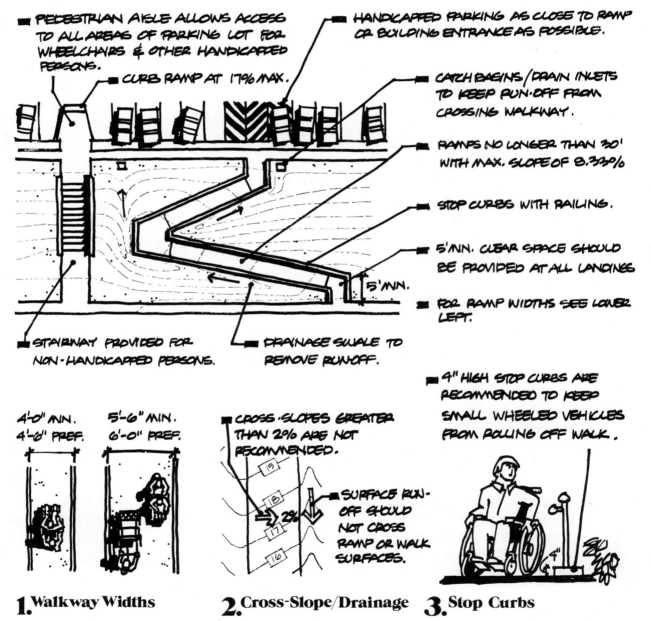

- PEDESTRIAN AISLE ALLOWS ACCESS TO ALL AREAS OF PARKING LOT FOR WHEELCHAIRS & OTHER HANDICAPPED PERSONS.

- CURB RAMP AT 17% MAX.

- HANDICAPPED PARKING AS CLOSE TO RAMP OR BUILDING ENTRANCE AS POSSIBLE.

- CATCH BASINS/DRAIN INLETS TO KEEP RUN-OFF FROM CROSSING WALKWAY.

- RAMPS NO LONGER THAN 30' WITH MAX. SLOPE OF 8.33%

- STOP CURBS WITH RAILING.

- 5' MIN. CLEAR SPACE SHOULD BE PROVIDED AT ALL LANDINGS

- FOR RAMP WIDTHS SEE LOWER LEFT.

5' MIN.

- STAIRWAY PROVIDED FOR NON-HANDICAPPED PERSONS.

- DRAINAGE SWALE TO REMOVE RUNOFF.

- 4" HIGH STOP CURBS ARE RECOMMENDED TO KEEP SMALL WHEELED VEHICLES FROM ROLLING OFF WALK.

4'-0" MIN.
4'-6" PREF.

5'-6" MIN.
6'-0" PREF.

- CROSS-SLOPES GREATER THAN 2% ARE NOT RECOMMENDED.

2%

- SURFACE RUN-OFF SHOULD NOT CROSS RAMP OR WALK SURFACES.

**1.** Walkway Widths

**2.** Cross-Slope/Drainage

**3.** Stop Curbs

concrete curbs are simply an unavoidable necessity, and from municipalities who further aggravate the problem by writing in curbing clauses to building ordinances for no other reason than that it has always been a past requirement. While this section by no means advocates the retraction of municipal curbing requirements, it does seem that viable alternatives should be allowed where they would reduce potential barriers and hazards while still satisfying existing requirements.

When specifying the use of conventional curbing, the designer should be aware of the following items:

1. Curbing should not create any unnecessary barriers to physically handicapped individuals. Where barriers have been created, previously laid curbs should either be removed or ramped.

2. Curbing, if necessary, should never be higher than the maximum height of one step; 6½". This is particularly important where there is any pedestrian traffic crossing over, or vehicles parking adjacent to the curb.

3. "Double" or "stepped" curbs are difficult for the handicapped to negotiate, and in darkness are hazardous to all pedestrians. Their use should be limited, if not restricted.

## Intersections

Any discussion on walkways would be incomplete without some mention of intersections and the potential hazards they can cause for handicapped people moving through the environment. Essentially, there are three items pertaining to intersections about which the designer should be concerned: (1) Vehicular and Pedestrian Warning Systems; (2) Pedestrian Crosswalks; (3) Directional and Informative Signage.

1. **Warning Systems:**
   a. Where there is a great deal of vehicular and

# Curb Ramps

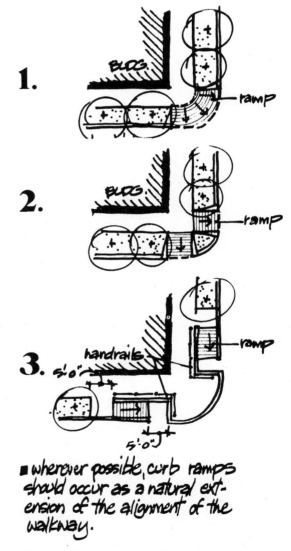

■ wherever possible, curb ramps should occur as a natural extension of the alignment of the walkway.

## Curb Ramps at Corners

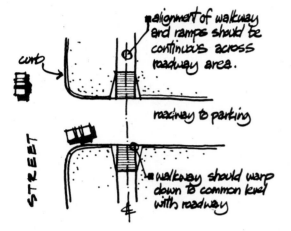

alignment of walkway and ramps should be continuous across roadway area.

curb

roadway to parking

■ walkway should warp down to common level with roadway

STREET

**Alignment of Ramps**

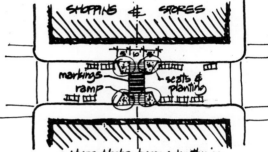

SHOPPING & STORES

markings

seats & planting

ramp

■ Where blocks become lengthy in areas of high pedestrian use, crossings at mid-block shorten required walking distance and reduce dangerous "jaywalking".

**Mid-Block Crossings**

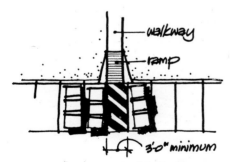

walkway

ramp

3'0" minimum

■ access to curb cut and walkway must be kept clear of parked cars. Area should be clearly marked for visability.

**Access to Ramps**

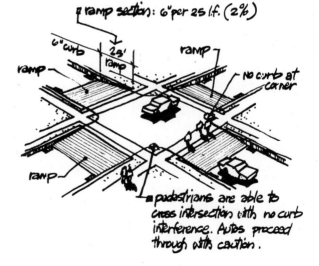

■ ramp section: 6" per 25 l.f. (2%)

6" curb

25' ramp

ramp

ramp

no curb at corner

ramp

■ pedestrians are able to cross intersection with no curb interference. Autos proceed through with caution.

**Ramped Intersection**

33

# Curb Ramps

■ avoid "lip" greater than ½" wherever ramp meets adjacent paving at top or bottom.

max. gradient 17%

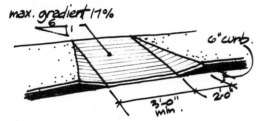

6" curb.
3'-0" min.
2'-0"

**1. Flared Ramp**

■ corrugated lines in ramps should be avoided since they can hold water in freezing weather and become icy.

max. gradient 17%

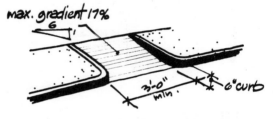

3'-0" min.
6" curb

**2. Ramp With Continuous Curb**

■ use of this type often interferes with curb-side storm drainage & snow plowing.

max. gradient 17%

side slopes "feathered" @ 8% max.
3'-0" min.
6"

**3. Extended Ramp**

■ locate handrail to avoid conflict with adjacent pedestrian walkway.

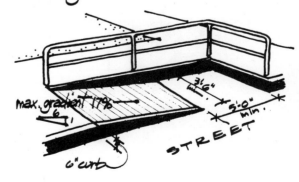

max. gradient 17%
3'-6"
5'-0" min.
STREET
6" curb

**4. Parallel Ramp**

# Curb Types

## Comments

**1. Vertical Face Curb**

a. HEIGHTS GREATER THAN 6" ARE AWKWARD FOR HANDICAPPED AND OTHERS.
b. REQUIRES CURB CUT RAMP FOR WHEELCHAIR.
c. CONTRASTING COLOR TO ADJACENT PAVEMENT INCREASES VISABILITY.

**2. Sloped Face Curb**

a. HEIGHTS GREATER THAN 6" ARE AWKWARD.
b. PROVIDE CURB RAMP FOR WHEELCHAIRS.
c. SLOPING FACE MAY PRESENT HAZARDOUS SURFACE IF STEPPED UPON.
d. CONTRAST COLOR WITH ADJACENT PAVEMENT.

**3. Pre-Made Wheel Stops Stops**

a. STANDARD LENGTH 8'-0".
b. ANCHOR SECURELY TO PAVEMENT TO AVOID MIS-ALIGNMENT.
c. PROVIDE MIN. 32" CLEAR SPACE BETWEEN UNITS FOR WHEELCHAIRS AND OTHERS.
d. CONTRAST COLOR WITH ADJACENT PAVEMENT.

**4. Posts and Bollards**

a. 2'-0" HT. MIN. FOR VISABILITY FROM APPROACHING VEHICLES.
b. ANCHOR SECURELY TO PAVEMENT TO AVOID MIS-ALIGNMENT.
c. PROVIDE MIN. 32" CLEAR SPACE BETWEEN UNITS FOR WHEELCHAIRS AND OTHERS.
d. CONTRAST COLOR WITH ADJACENT PAVEMENT.

**5. Guard Rails**

a. PROVIDES MAX. CONTROL OF VEHICLES.
b. 2'-0" HT. MIN. FOR VISABILITY FROM VEHICLES.
c. USEFUL ALONG PERIMETERS OF ROADWAY OR PARKING AREAS.
d. PROVIDE OPENINGS FOR WHEELCHAIRS AND OTHERS WHERE NECESSARY, 32" MIN.

**6. Posts and Chains**

a. HAZARDOUS IF CHAIN SAGS BELOW 32" OR HIGHER THAN 42"
b. PROVIDE MIN. 32" CLEAR SPACE BETWEEN UNITS WHERE NECESSARY.
c. CONTRAST COLOR WITH ADJACENT PAVEMENT.

# Curb Cuts and Intersections

- SEPERATED CURB CUTS LEAVE WALK SPACE AT CORNERS FOR STREET SIGNS, UTILITY POLES, ETC.
- PROVIDES GOOD ORIENTATION FOR THE BLIND WHEN LOCATED IN LINE WITH PEDESTRIAN WALKWAYS.

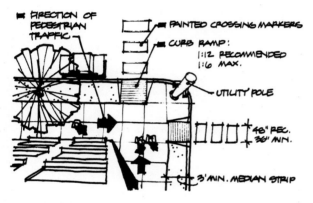

- DIRECTION OF PEDESTRIAN TRAFFIC
- PAINTED CROSSING MARKERS
- CURB RAMP: 1:12 RECOMMENDED 1:6 MAX.
- UTILITY POLE
- 48" REC. 36" MIN.
- 3' MIN. MEDIAN STRIP

## 1. Seperated

- CONTINUOUS CURB CUTS ARE USEFUL WHERE CORNER SPACE IS LIMITED.
- RAMPED SURFACES ARE PROVIDED FOR PEDESTRIANS CROSSING DIAGONALLY AS WELL AS PERPENDICULAR.

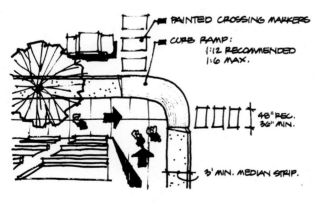

- PAINTED CROSSING MARKERS
- CURB RAMP: 1:12 RECOMMENDED 1:6 MAX.
- 48" REC. 36" MIN.
- 3' MIN. MEDIAN STRIP.

## 2. Continuous

- OFF-SET CURB CUTS WORK WELL WHERE LARGE NUMBERS OF PEDESTRIANS MUST QUICKLY CROSS BUSY STREETS. MOVING CURB RAMPS AWAY FROM CORNER INCREASES PEDESTRIAN AISLE WIDTHS.

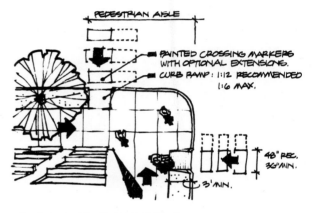

- PEDESTRIAN AISLE
- PAINTED CROSSING MARKERS WITH OPTIONAL EXTENSIONS.
- CURB RAMP: 1:12 RECOMMENDED 1:6 MAX.
- 48" REC. 36" MIN.
- 3' MIN.

## 3. Seperated and Off-Set

# Curb Cut Considerations

■ WHERE POSSIBLE, KEEP CURB RAMPS FROM PENETRATING WALKWAY SURFACES BY USE OF MEDIAN STRIPS.

■ WHERE EXISTING WALKS ARE NARROW WITH NO ROOM FOR MEDIAN STRIPS, EXTEND CURB RAMP ACROSS FULL WIDTH OF WALK. *

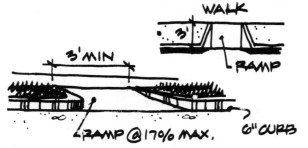

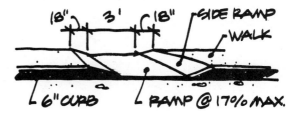

■ MEDIAN STRIPS BETWEEN WALKS AND ROAD: 3' MIN. RECOMMENDED.

* THIS SOLUTION IS FOR EXTREMELY CONFINED SPACES AND SHOULD NOT BE USED AS A GENERAL DESIGN SOLUTION.

## 1. General Dimensions

## 3. Narrow Urban Walks

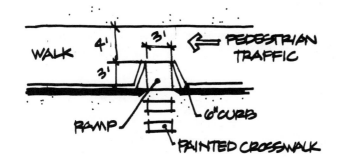

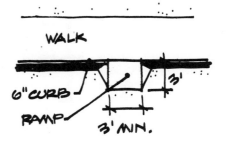

■ IN MANY URBAN SITUATIONS, RAMPS WILL EXTEND INTO WALKWAYS. A MIN. 4' OF WALKWAY SHOULD BE MAINTAINED BEHIND RAMPS TO HANDLE THROUGH PEDESTRIAN TRAFFIC.

■ RAMPS PROTRUDING INTO ROADWAYS ARE NOT RECOMMENDED FOR AREAS WHERE SNOW FALL IS PREVALENT. EXTENSION CAN BE DAMAGED BY PLOWS AND INHIBIT SNOW REMOVAL.

## 2. Urban Walks

## 4. Extended Curb Ramps

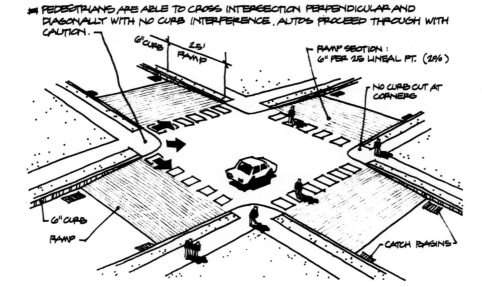

■ PEDESTRIANS ARE ABLE TO CROSS INTERSECTION PERPENDICULAR AND DIAGONALLY WITH NO CURB INTERFERENCE. AUTOS PROCEED THROUGH WITH CAUTION.

6" CURB    25' RAMP

RAMP SECTION: 6" PER 25 LINEAL FT. (2%)

NO CURB CUT AT CORNERS

6" CURB RAMP

CATCH BASINS

## 4. Flush/On-Grade Intersections

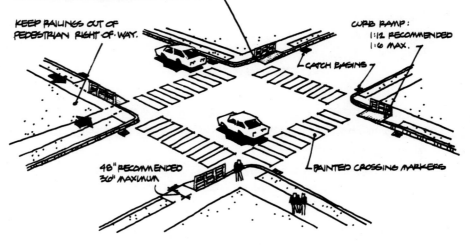

■ FENCED CURB CUTS ARE USEFUL IN URBAN CONDITIONS WHERE WALKWAYS ARE TOO NARROW TO ALLOW CURB RAMPS TO BE PLACED PERPENDICULAR TO ROADWAYS AS IN DRAWINGS 1 THROUGH 3. RAILINGS ARE ADDED TO KEEP PEDESTRIANS FROM TRIPPING OVER THE STEEP SIDEWALL BETWEEN RAMPS AND WALK.

KEEP RAILINGS OUT OF PEDESTRIAN RIGHT-OF-WAY.

CURB RAMP: 1:12 RECOMMENDED 1:6 MAX.

CATCH BASINS

48" RECOMMENDED 36" MAXIMUM

PAINTED CROSSING MARKERS

## 5. Intersections with Fenced Curb Cuts

# Pedestrian Crossings

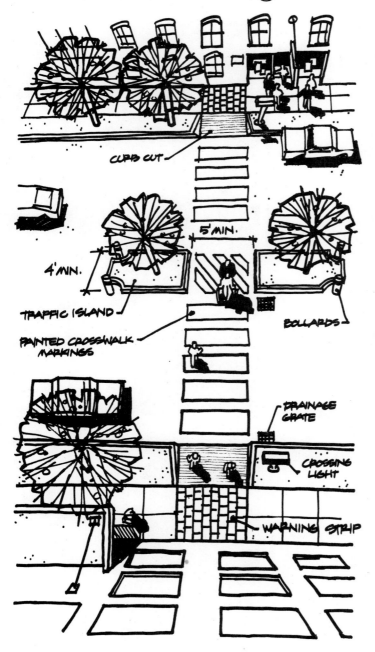

CURB CUT

5' MIN.

4' MIN.

TRAFFIC ISLAND

PAINTED CROSSWALK MARKINGS

BOLLARDS

DRAINAGE GRATE

CROSSING LIGHT

WARNING STRIP

- AT BUSY CROSSINGS, A BUZZER SHOULD SOUND SO LONG AS THE PEDESTRIAN LIGHT IS AT "WALK."

- ALLOW SUFFICIENT TIME FOR SAFE CROSSING; 1 YARD/SECOND RECOMMENDED.

- PUSH BUTTONS TO ACTIVATE PEDESTRIAN CROSSING LIGHT SHOULD BE AT AN ACCESSIBLE HEIGHT TO BOTH CHILDREN & PERSONS IN WHEELCHAIRS.

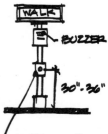

WALK

BUZZER

30"-36"

PUSH BUTTON

- PASSAGE THROUGH PEDESTRIAN ISLANDS SHOULD BE 5' MIN. WIDTH FOR TWO-WAY TRAFFIC, AND FLUSH WITH ROADWAY SURFACE.

- TRAFFIC ISLANDS SHOULD BE 4' MIN. WIDTH TO PROTECT STRANDED PEDESTRIANS FROM VEHICULAR TRAFFIC.

- CURB CUTS AT 17% MAX. SLOPE AND 5' MIN. WIDTH FOR 2 WAY TRAFFIC.

- DRAINAGE GRATES SHOULD BE LOCATED AWAY FROM PEDESTRIAN PATHS, ESPECIALLY WHERE WATER MAY BACK-UP ACROSS WALKWAYS AND FREEZE DURING WINTER MONTHS. GRATE OPENINGS SHOULD BE KEPT TO A MAX. OF 3/4" SQ.

- CONTRASTING PAVING MATERIAL CAN BE PLACED BEHIND CURB CUTS TO ACT AS WARNING STRIPS FOR THE BLIND. PAVING SHOULD EXTEND FULL WIDTH OF WALKWAY.

# Wheel-Stop and Post Layout

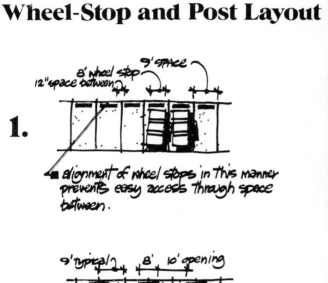

**1.** alignment of wheel stops in this manner prevents easy access through space between.

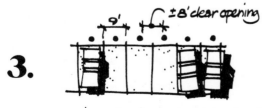

**2.** alignment in this manner allows greater opening between stops and requires ½ as many, however requires parking space delineation.

**3.** posts or barriers should be located on the center of the parking space to allow pedestrian movements in the aisle between.

PARKING RESTRICTED TO WHEELCHAIR PERSONNEL

pedestrian traffic at intersections, signal lights should be used to assist people in crossing the street.

**b.** For safety reasons, traffic signals should be designed so that glare from the sun does not interfere with their ability to be seen, nor should they be placed where they are easily confused with the surrounding background.

**c.** The configuration of the lights should always be arranged with the red to the top, amber in the center, and green at the bottom; this is the only way colorblind people have of determining when it is safe to cross.

**d.** In addition to the vehicular signal, pedestrian "walk" — "don't walk" signals are helpful. Crossing signs should be placed where they are plainly visible, and if push-buttons are incorporated into the system, they should be located no higher than 3'-6".

**e.** Plant materials or other obstacles should never be allowed to visually block pedestrian movements from motorists or vehicular movements from pedestrians.

## 2. Crosswalks:

Crosswalks are used to delineate an aisle for pedestrian traffic to use when traveling through an intersection against vehicular traffic.

**a.** Crosswalks should be constructed so as to be easily seen by motorists.

**b.** A variety of visual and textural materials can be used for crosswalk delineation.

**c.** The interior width of a crosswalk should be as wide as the width of the approaching walk.

**d.** The use of textured warning strips for the blind at crosswalks is not recommended. (See "Signage Considerations, 'Textural Paving'").

## 3. Signage:

Most problems relating to signage at intersections can be attributed to either size or graphic layout. When considering signage to be posted at intersections, the designer should:

**a.** Make sure locations are easily visible to either motorist or pedestrians, depending on who the sign is intended for.

**b.** Choose sign sizes relative to specific design situations. This is particularly critical for motorists; when speeds increase, visibility decreases.

**c.** Whenever possible, use signs that have dark colored backgrounds with light colored letters. Research has proven that this combination is easier to read than dark colored letters on light backgrounds.

■ in areas where people are likely to be carrying bulky items, guardrails, posts and curbs should be high enough to be easily seen; otherwise they can be a tripping hazard.

guard rail too low to be easily seen.

# Barrier Visability

# Catch Basin Considerations

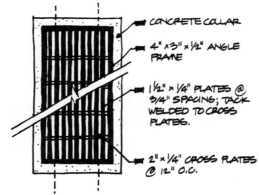

- CONCRETE COLLAR
- 4" x 3" x 1/2" ANGLE FRAME
- 1 1/2" x 1/4" PLATES @ 3/4" SPACING; TACK WELDED TO CROSS PLATES.
- 2" x 1/4" CROSS PLATES @ 12" O.C.

**1. Plan View**

ALWAYS LOCATE DRAINS PERPENDICULAR TO DIRECTION OF VEHICULAR AND PEDESTRIAN TRAFFIC.

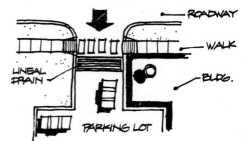

- ROADWAY
- WALK
- BLDG.
- LINEAL DRAIN
- PARKING LOT

LINEAL DRAINS ARE USED IN AREAS WHERE STANDARD CATCH BASINS CAN NOT HANDLE SHEET DRAINAGE.

**3. Plan Layout**

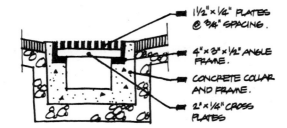

- 1 1/2" x 1/4" PLATES @ 3/4" SPACING.
- 4" x 3" x 1/2" ANGLE FRAME.
- CONCRETE COLLAR AND FRAME.
- 2" x 1/4" CROSS PLATES

**2. Cross-Section**

44

# Ramps, Stairs, and Handrails

## Outdoor Ramps

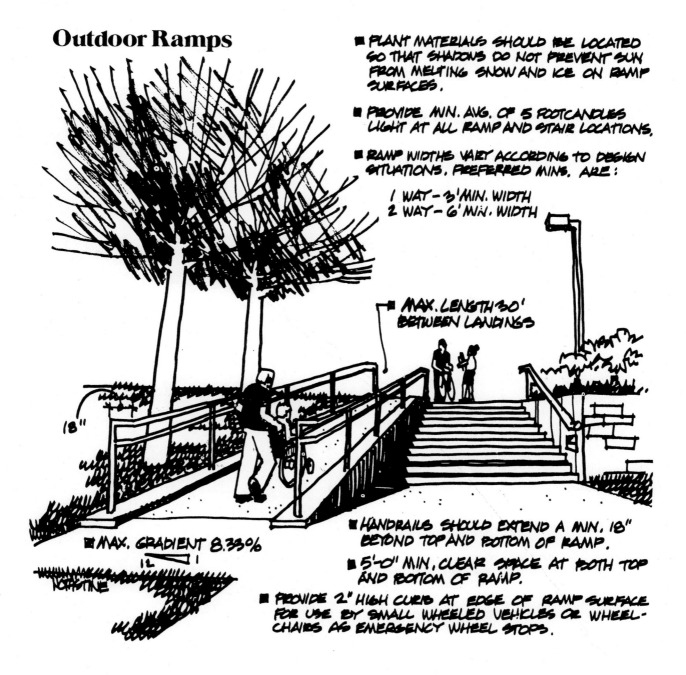

■ PLANT MATERIALS SHOULD BE LOCATED SO THAT SHADOWS DO NOT PREVENT SUN FROM MELTING SNOW AND ICE ON RAMP SURFACES.

■ PROVIDE MIN. AVG. OF 5 FOOTCANDLES LIGHT AT ALL RAMP AND STAIR LOCATIONS.

■ RAMP WIDTHS VARY ACCORDING TO DESIGN SITUATIONS. PREFERRED MINS. ARE:

1 WAY - 3' MIN. WIDTH
2 WAY - 6' MIN. WIDTH

■ MAX. LENGTH 30' BETWEEN LANDINGS

18"

■ MAX. GRADIENT 8.33%

1L / 1

NORMALINE

■ HANDRAILS SHOULD EXTEND A MIN. 18" BEYOND TOP AND BOTTOM OF RAMP.

■ 5'-0" MIN. CLEAR SPACE AT BOTH TOP AND BOTTOM OF RAMP.

■ PROVIDE 2" HIGH CURB AT EDGE OF RAMP SURFACE FOR USE BY SMALL WHEELED VEHICLES OR WHEEL-CHAIRS AS EMERGENCY WHEEL STOPS.

## Outdoor Ramps

Ramps are alternate routes for people who are not able to use stairs; however, they do not take the place of stairs since certain portions of the population find ramps more difficult to use. Any surface pitched above 5% is considered a ramp.

1. The maximum gradient for a ramp of any extended length should not exceed 1:12 (8.33%), not including curb ramps.

2. The maximum length for a single ramp at 1:12 should not exceed 30'-0". Ramps of lesser grades can, of course, be lengthened.

3. The minimum clear width of any ramp is 3'-0". Where ramps are heavily used by pedestrians and service deliveries, there should be sufficient width to accommodate both, or provisions made for alternate routes.

4. The bottom and top approach to a ramp should be clear and level for a distance of at least 5'-0", allowing for turning maneuvers by strollers, dollies, wheelchairs, etc.

5. A textural signal prior to the ramp, at both top and bottom, may be used to warn the pedestrian of the upcoming obstacle. (See "Signage Considerations, 'Textural Paving'" for details.)

6. Ramps should be designed to carry a minimum live load of 100 lbs. per square foot.

7. Low curbs along the sides of ramps and landings should be provided as surfaces against which wheeled vehicles can turn their wheels in order to stop.

8. Ramps should be illuminated to an average maintained light level which insures their safe use in darkness. It is important that the heel and toe of the ramp be particularly well illuminated.

9. Ramps should be maintained properly to keep them from being hazardous. Debris, snow and ice should be kept off the surface. Handrails should, at all times, be properly secured.

# Ramps for Outdoor Use

## 1. Straight-Run

ramp

landing

5' min.
30' max.
5' min.
30' max.
5' min.

1 way 3'
2 way 6'

## 2. Angled Landing

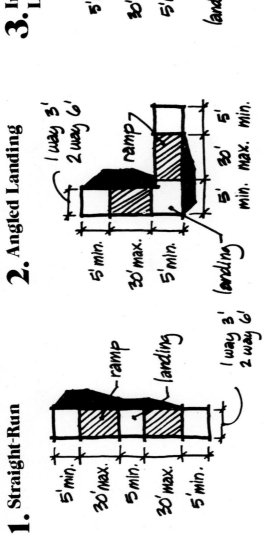

ramp

landing

5' min.
30' max.
5' min.

1 way 3'
2 way 6'

1 way 3'
2 way 6'

5'
min.
30'
max.
5'
min.

## 3. Intermediate/Switch-Back Landing

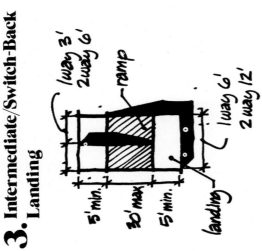

ramp

landing

5' min.
30' max.
5' min.

1 way 3'
2 way 6'

1 way 6'
2 way 12'

# Conditions at Tops & Bases of Ramps

## 1. Traffic Goes Straight

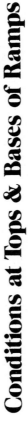

landing

5' min.

ramp

## 2. Traffic Turns

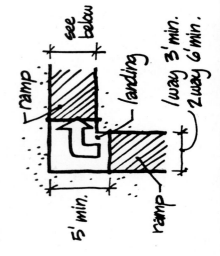

ramp

landing

5' min.

see below

ramp

1 way 3' min.
2 way 6' min.

## 3. Traffic Turns to Gate/Doorway

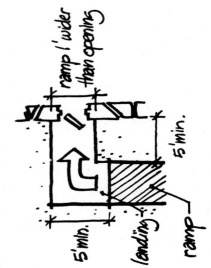

ramp 1' wider than opening

5' min.

landing

5' min.

ramp

# Ramp Considerations from Various Organizations

- WALKWAYS EXCEEDING 5% GRADES SHOULD BE CONSIDERED RAMPS.
- UPPER RAILS PROVIDED FOR GENERAL USE.

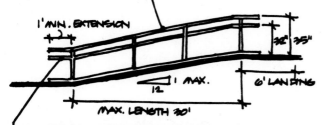

1' MIN. EXTENSION

32" 35"

1 MAX.
12

6' LANDING

MAX. LENGTH 30'

- LOWER RAILS PROVIDED FOR WHEELCHAIR USERS AND CHILDREN.

## 1. American Standards/Goldsmith

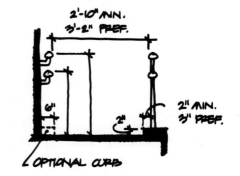

2'-10" MIN.
3'-2" PREF.

6"

2"

2" MIN.
3" PREF.

OPTIONAL CURB

- 2" HIGH CURBS SHOULD BE PROVIDED ALONG RAMP EDGES AS EMERGENCY WHEELSTOPS.

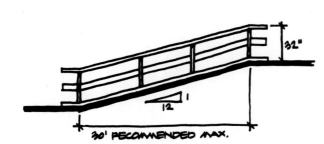

32"

1
12

30' RECOMMENDED MAX.

## 2. National Park Service

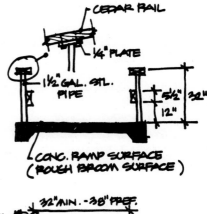

CEDAR RAIL

¼" PLATE

1½" GAL. STL. PIPE

5½" 32"
12"

32" MIN. - 38" PREF.

4"

24" 32"

2"

CONC. RAMP SURFACE
(ROUGH BROOM SURFACE)

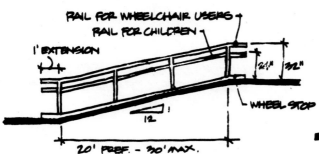

RAIL FOR WHEELCHAIR USERS
RAIL FOR CHILDREN

1' EXTENSION

24" 32"

1
12

WHEEL STOP

20' PREF. - 30' MAX.

- 1½" MIN. - 2" DESIRABLE OUTSIDE DIAMETER FOR HANDRAILS.

## 3. H.U.D. - "Housing for the Physically Impaired"

# Outdoor Stairways

■ SHADOWS FROM ADJACENT PLANTINGS SHOULD NOT PREVENT THE SUN FROM MELTING ICE AND SNOW.

■ PROVIDE A MINIMUM AVERAGE OF 5 FOOTCANDLES LIGHT AT ALL STAIRWAY LOCATIONS.

■ SURFACE OF ALL TREADS SHOULD BE NON-SLIP AND PITCHED FORWARD AT 1/8" PER FOOT TO DRAIN SURFACE WATER. PROVIDE 3/4" CHAMFER OR 1" ROUNDING TO NOSING OF ALL TREADS.

■ COLOR OF STAIRS SHOULD CONTRAST WITH ADJACENT PAVING.

■ CHEEKWALLS AT SAME GRADE LEVEL AS ADJACENT LAWN ELIMINATES NEED FOR HAND TRIMMING OF GRASS.

■ SEE | HANDRAILS | FOR ADDITIONAL INFORMATION.

■ STAIRWAYS WIDTHS SHOULD BE DETERMINED BY THE PROJECTED AMOUNT OF PEDESTRIAN TRAFFIC AND THE WIDTHS OF APPROACHING WALKWAYS. PREFERRED MINIMUMS ARE:

    1 WAY- 3' MINIMUM WIDTH
    2 WAY- 5' MINIMUM WIDTH

■ HANDRAILS SHOULD EXTEND BEYOND THE TOP AND BOTTOM STEP A MINIMUM OF 18"

■ CHEEKWALLS SHOULD EXTEND BENEATH HANDRAILS AN EQUAL DISTANCE.

## Outdoor Stairs

Stairs should be designed to provide for the minimum amount of energy expenditure, a factor which is particularly important to elderly and semi-ambulant people. They should be wide enough for people to pass one another, be of safe design, and have proper appurtenances to ensure their safe use.

1. The minimum clear width for any stairway should be 3'-0''. Where stairs are heavily used, widths should be increased to handle traffic requirements.

2. The maximum rise between landings for external unprotected stairs is 4'-0''. Where the stairs are protected, a 6'-0'' rise is acceptable. Stairs should not be used where there are only a few in a series. These are dangerous and usually not necessary.

3. All steps in a series should have uniform tread width and riser height.

4. Stair treads should be deep enough to allow a man to place his whole foot on it. The preferred range is between 11'' to 14½''.

5. Risers for exterior stairs should be between 4'' to 6½'' in height, with 5¾'' being preferred.

6. Nosings should be rounded or chamfered. A 1'' rounded nosing is most acceptable. It should be of a color contrasting that of the treads and risers to make identification easier. Abrupt, square nosings provide less frictional resistance and cause tripping.

7. Stairways should have an average maintained light level which insures their safe use in darkness. Light should be cast down toward risers so that the treads will not be in shadow. (For recommended lighting levels see "Lighting" section.)

## Outdoor Step Types

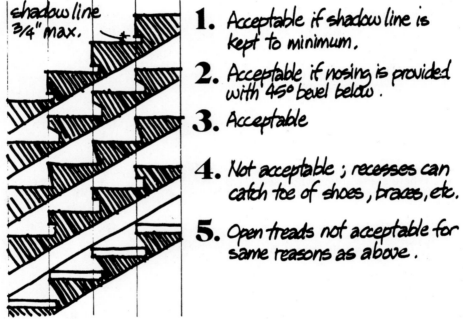

**shadow line 3/4" max.**

**1.** Acceptable if shadow line is kept to minimum.

**2.** Acceptable if nosing is provided with 45° bevel below.

**3.** Acceptable

**4.** Not acceptable; recesses can catch toe of shoes, braces, etc.

**5.** Open treads not acceptable for same reasons as above.

## Outdoor Steps Rules-of-Thumb

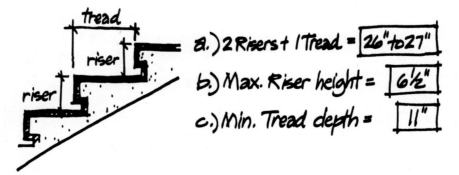

**tread**

**riser**

**riser**

a.) 2 Risers + 1 Tread = 26" to 27"

b.) Max. Riser height = 6½"

c.) Min. Tread depth = 11"

# Outdoor Landings

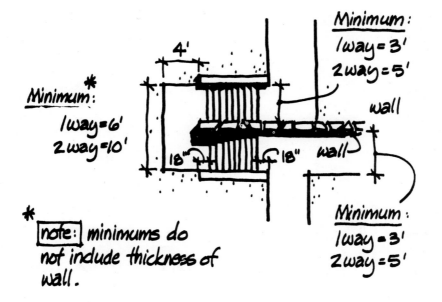

Minimum:
1 way = 3'
2 way = 5'

wall

4'

Minimum: *
1 way = 6'
2 way = 10'

18"    18"    wall    wall

Minimum
1 way = 3'
2 way = 5'

\* note: minimums do not include thickness of wall.

# Height Between Landings

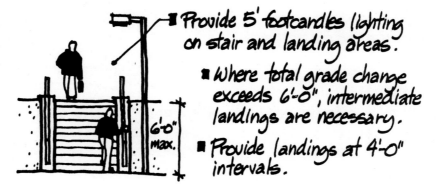

6'-0" max.

- Provide 5' footcandles lighting on stair and landing areas.

- Where total grade change exceeds 6'-0", intermediate landings are necessary.

- Provide landings at 4'-0" intervals.

# Stairway Considerations

- TREAD WIDTHS FOR STAIRWAYS ARE FOUND USING THE FOLLOWING FORMULA:

$$2 \times \text{RISER HEIGHT} + \text{TREAD WIDTH} = 24 - 26 \text{ INCHES}$$

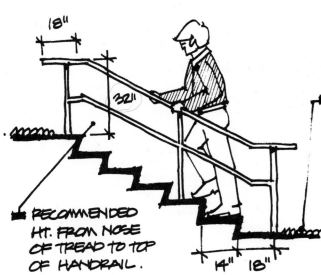

- RECOMMENDED HT. FROM NOSE OF TREAD TO TOP OF HANDRAIL.

- HANDRAILS SECURELY FIXED BECAUSE OF ABNORMAL LOADS ACTING IN DIFFERENT DIRECTIONS.

- STAIRWAY WIDTHS SHOULD BE DETERMINED BY PROPOSED TRAFFIC VOLUMES:  3' MIN. ONE·WAY
  5' MIN. TWO·WAY

- ANTI-SLIP STRIP AT NOSE OF EACH TREAD.

- RISERS AND TREADS IN CONTRASTING COLORS FOR INCREASED VISIBILITY.

1" OVERHANG

- TEXTURAL WARNING STRIP FOR BLIND PERSONS IS RECOMMENDED AT TOP AND BOTTOM LANDING.*

* [THE VALUE OF THIS PRACTICE IS QUESTIONABLE BECAUSE OF THE LACK OF OVERALL STANDARDIZATION.]

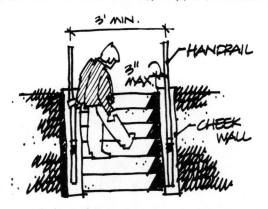

HANDRAIL

CHEEK WALL

- STAIRWAY WIDTHS SHOULD CONSIDER THE NEEDS OF SEMI·AMBULANT PEOPLE WITH LEG BRACES WHO MUST SWING LEGS OUT WHEN CLIMBING STAIRS.

# Handrail Cross-Sections

■ Do not allow hands to use natural opposing grip; usually because rail is too wide.

1½"-2" preferrable

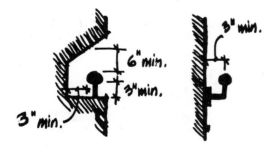

■ Allow hands to use natural, opposing grip.

6" min.
3" min.
3" min.
3" min.

■ All edges should be chamfered or rounded off, also keep wall surfaces smooth to limit cuts and scrapes.

# Cheek-Walls

## 1. Recessed

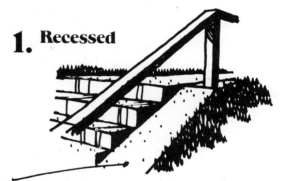

■ Recessed cheek walls allow stairs to drain freely or be swept clean of debris or snow; can be hazardous if person steps off edge of stairs.

## 2. Raised

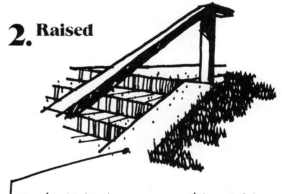

■ Raised cheekwalls provide safety from stepping off stair edge, but tend to collect snow and debris.

# Handrails for Ramps

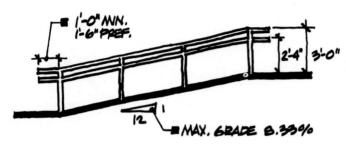

- 3'-0" IS THE MOST COMFORTABLE HT. FOR HANDRAILS ON RAMPS.

- A SECOND HANDRAIL, USEFUL TO PEOPLE IN WHEELCHAIRS AND CHILDREN SHOULD BE PLACED AT 2'-4".

- HANDRAILS SHOULD EXTEND A MIN. 1'-0" BEYOND BOTH ENDS OF A RAMP.

# Handrails for Stairways

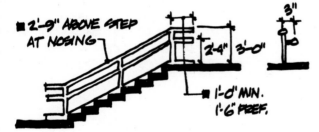

- 3'-0" IS THE MOST COMFORTABLE HT. FOR RAILINGS AT BOTH ENDS OF STAIRWAYS. 2'-9" IS THE ACCEPTED HT. ON STAIRWAYS.

- A SECOND HANDRAIL, USEFUL TO CHILDREN SHOULD BE PLACED AT 2'-4"

- HANDRAILS SHOULD EXTEND A MIN. OF 1'-0" BEYOND STAIRWAYS.

# Handrails for Extra-Wide Stairways

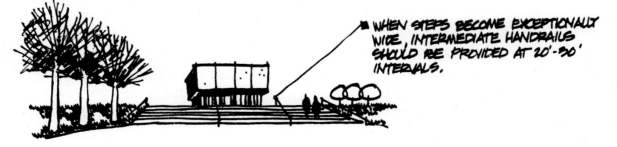

- WHEN STEPS BECOME EXCEPTIONALLY WIDE, INTERMEDIATE HANDRAILS SHOULD BE PROVIDED AT 20'-30' INTERVALS.

# Handrails for Outdoor Use

Handrails serve the primary function of providing support for people who are in the process of climbing or descending stairs or ramps; whereas railings are placed more for reasons of preventing people from entering or falling into a dangerous area.

The designer should take into account the following items in regard to handrails and railings:

1. **General:**
   **a.** Handrails and railings should preferably be round or oval, 1½" to 2" in diameter.
   **b.** There should be a minimum 3" spacing between handrails and adjacent walls, and wall surfaces should preferably be non-abrasive.
   **c.** Where handrails or railings are fully recessed into walls, a space of 6" should be allowed between the top of the rail and the top of the recess, and a space of 3" should be allowed between the bottom of the rail and the bottom of the recess.
   **d.** The ends of handrails should be rounded off or turned into the wall so that they are not hazardous.
   **e.** Handrails, railings, and their appurtenances should be maintained free of slivers, sharp protrusions, etc.

2. **Handrails for Ramps:**
   **a.** Handrails should be provided on both sides of every ramp. They should extend past the heel and toe, 1'-0" to 1'-6", except in places where the extension in itself presents a hazard.
   **b.** The vertical dimension from the ramp surface to the top of a single handrail should be between 2'-8" and 3'-0".
   **c.** A second rail is advantageous to children and wheelchair dependent people. Where two rails are used, the top rail should be placed at 3'-0" to 3'-3", and the lower rail should be placed at 2'-4".

   **d.** Handrails should be continuous across the landings.
   **e.** Handrails should be designed to support 250 lbs. and be kept securely fastened at all times.

3. **Handrails for Stairs:**
   **a.** Handrails should be placed on each side of a stairway and should be 2'-9" vertically from the nose of the treads to the top of the handrail; the distance from the landing surface to the top of the handrail should be 2'-8" to 3'-0".
   **b.** Handrails should extend past the tread at top and bottom, a length of 2'-0" to 3'-6" unless the extension in and of itself creates a hazard. The change of direction of the handrail provides a tactile clue to a person about to make the last step. Where the extension of the handrail is of itself a hazard, notches or knurling on the rail may be used to provide the clue.
   **c.** Handrails should be continuous across landings where possible.
   **d.** Handrails should be designed to support 250 lbs. and should be kept securely fastened at all times.

## Handrail Cross-Sections

■ HANDRAILS SHOULD ALLOW THE HAND TO USE ITS NATURAL OPPOSING GRIP.

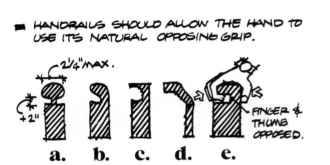

■ HANDRAILS a - e ARE ACCEPTABLE BECAUSE THEY ALLOW FINGERS AND THUMB TO FORM AN OPPOSING GRIP.

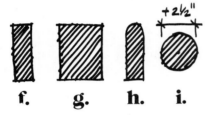

■ HANDRAILS f - i ARE NOT ACCEPTABLE BECAUSE THEY DO NOT ALLOW HAND TO FORM AN OPPOSING GRIP.

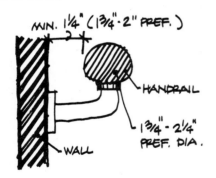

■ HANDRAILS MOUNTED ALONG WALLS SHOULD BE OFF-SET A MIN. DISTANCE OF 1¼" TO PREVENT SCRAPED KNUCKLES AND REDUCE THE CHANCES OF ARMS PINIONING IN THE EVENT OF A FALL.

# Walls, Gates, Fences, and Railings

## Walls as Seating Surfaces

- DULL AND LIGHT COLORED MATERIALS ARE GENERALLY COOLER SURFACES TO SIT ON WHEN IN DIRECT SUNLIGHT. DARK AND SHINY SURFACES TEND TO BECOME UNCOMFORTABLY HOT WHEN IN DIRECT SUNLIGHT, AND CONSEQUENTLY ARE BETTER USED IN SHADED LOCATIONS.

- VEGETATION NEAR SITTING AREAS SHOULD NOT CONFLICT WITH PEOPLE SEATED IN THE AREA OR PASSING THROUGH IT. SPECIES THAT ARE INVASIVE, INJURIOUS, OR DROP EXCESSIVE DEBRIS SHOULD BE AVOIDED OR USED WITH DISCRETION.

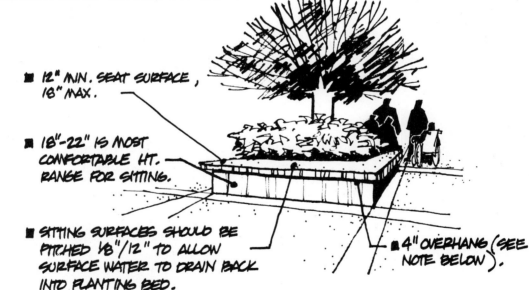

- 12" MIN. SEAT SURFACE, 18" MAX.

- 18"-22" IS MOST COMFORTABLE HT. RANGE FOR SITTING.

- SITTING SURFACES SHOULD BE PITCHED 1/8"/12" TO ALLOW SURFACE WATER TO DRAIN BACK INTO PLANTING BED.

- 4" OVERHANG (SEE NOTE BELOW).

- 4" OVERHANG PROVIDES SPACE FOR HEELS, WHICH MAKES SITTING MORE COMFORTABLE. ALSO ALLOWS PEOPLE TO PLACE THEIR HEELS MORE DIRECTLY BENEATH THEIR CENTER OF GRAVITY, WHICH IN TURN MAKES RISING UP OUT OF A SEATED POSITION EASIER.

- LOWER HEIGHTS BECOME INCREASINGLY DIFFICULT FOR MANY HANDICAPPED PEOPLE TO SIT INTO AND RISE OUT OF.

- 2'-0" LEG SPACE SHOULD BE PROVIDED SO THAT SEATED PEDESTRIANS DON'T BLOCK ADJACENT WALKWAYS.

# Walls

In addition to their common functions of retaining earth and separating site elements, walls can be designed to provide a number of secondary functions such as seating, surfaces on which to rest packages, and support and guidance to physically restricted people.

When designing seat walls, retaining walls, and free-standing walls, the designer should consider the following items:

1. **Seat Walls:**
   a. Seat walls should be between 18" and 22" high in order to accommodate physically restricted people. Walls lower than this present a hazard as they are easily overlooked.
   b. A width of at least 12" is required for comfortable seating on the top surface of any wall.

2. **Low Retaining Walls:**
   a. Retaining walls between 2'-0" and 3'-0" are useful in providing surfaces to lean against in a half-sitting position, or as a surface to sit upon. Wheelchair users can easily rest packages on walls of this height.
   b. Walls between 3'-0" and 4'-0" in height are particularly good for package rests. They are difficult for most people to sit on, however.
   c. Where pedestrian or bicycle traffic occurs adjacent to the top of a wall, a barrier should be incorporated between the walkway and the edge to prevent people from inadvertently falling off. Barriers can be either a railing device or a natural hedge. See "Railings".

3. **High Retaining and Free-Standing Walls**
   a. These walls are above 4'-0" in height.
   b. Too high for seating, these walls are useful to the handicapped only with the addition of a handrail. Handrails should be located according to specifications in the "Handrail" section.

c. Where walls are located adjacent to walkways, weep holes should not be located so as to drain out onto the walking surface. Water drainage could form ice spots during winter months.

d. Drain pipes should not project past the face of any wall. Likewise, walls should be free of any projections or appendages which might prove dangerous to people passing by.

e. For inherent reasons of safety, all walls should be maintained in good condition.

# Gates

Gates used in the exterior environment should adhere to the same critical dimensions, design treatments, opening forces, etc., that apply to doors inside of a building since restricted people are obliged to use them in much the same manner.

Items to consider when designing gates are:

1. The minimum width dimension on a gate should never be less than 34" which, if one assumes a 2" thickness on the gate allows a 32" clear opening passageway when the gate is open.

2. The gate should have a latching mechanism that is operable by a lever or some other similar device.

3. Where a gate is likely to receive heavy use, a 16" high metal kickplate should be installed across its entire width. This is to prevent damage to the gate itself from crutches or wheelchair foot rests.

4. Where the gate has a self-closing mechanism, the force required to open it should not exceed 5 lbs. preferred (8 lbs maximum). The closing mechanism should also have a time delay to prevent the gate from closing too quickly on the person passing through it.

■ LOW WALLS ARE USEFUL AS SEATING FACILITIES, LEANING SUPPORTS, AND PACKAGE RESTS.

■ KEEP ADJACENT PLANT MATERIALS OFF OF SEAT AND OUT OF PEDESTRIAN WALKWAY.

SEAT TOP 12"

WALL HT. 3'-0" MAX.

■ PROVIDE 4"-6" CHANGE IN GRADE TO PREVENT WATER WASHING ONTO SEAT.

■ DRAINAGE FROM WEEP HOLES SHOULD NOT CAUSE HAZARD BY FREEZING ON WALKWAY.

■ TOP OF SEAT SHOULD BE PITCHED TOWARDS PLANTING BED AT $\frac{1}{8}$"/12" TO DRAIN SURFACE WATER.

# Wall Considerations

- A 3" DROP BEHIND SEAT WALLS IS RECOMMENDED TO KEEP DRAINAGE FROM RUNNING ONTO SEAT SURFACES.

- 8" RECOMMENDED SEAT WIDTH MIN. 12" PREFERRED

- 17"-18" RECOMMENDED SEAT HT. 20" MAX.

3"

24" MIN. LEG SPACE

## 1. Seat Walls

- A 12" SETBACK IS RECOMMENDED BETWEEN THE REAR OF WALLS AND ADJACENT SHRUBBERY.

12"

- 24" TO 28" HIGH WALLS ARE USEFUL AS REST SUPPORTS.

24" MIN. LEG SPACE

## 2. Low Retaining Walls

- PROVIDE 24" MIN. SPACE IN FRONT OF WALLS TO KEEP LEGS OFF ADJACENT WALKWAY. (36" FOR WHEELCHAIRS.)

- WALLS IN THE 36" TO 40" RANGE CAN BE USED AS ARM SUPPORTS.

SEE ABOVE.

## 3. Retaining Walls Above Waist Height

# Gate Recommendations

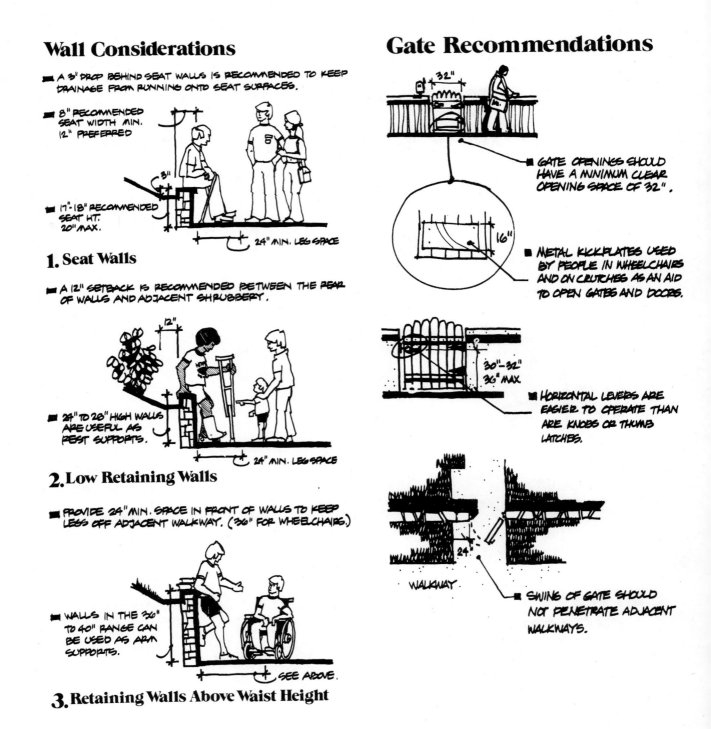

32"

16"

- GATE OPENINGS SHOULD HAVE A MINIMUM CLEAR OPENING SPACE OF 32".

- METAL KICKPLATES USED BY PEOPLE IN WHEELCHAIRS AND ON CRUTCHES AS AN AID TO OPEN GATES AND DOORS.

30"-32" 36" MAX.

- HORIZONTAL LEVERS ARE EASIER TO OPERATE THAN ARE KNOBS OR THUMB LATCHES.

WALKWAY

24

- SWING OF GATE SHOULD NOT PENETRATE ADJACENT WALKWAYS.

5. In some instances, an automatic opening mechanism may be helpful.

6. **Levers and Handles:**

   a. The use of knobs or mechanisms which require a grasping operation are not recommended since they are usable only by people with free hands and fingers. Knobs are also extremely difficult for people with partial or total manual handicaps to operate. Horizontal levers and handles should be used when and where possible since they are much easier to manipulate.

   b. Horizontal levers and handles should be placed preferably between 30" to 32" above the floor (36" maximum).

   c. Horizontal levers and handles are easier to grip by most people than are vertical ones.

7. **Baffles:**

   Baffles are commonly used for entries into restroom facilities or shelters. They serve the function of effectively blocking direct view into the facility without hindering access to it.

   The following items should be considered in the design of baffles:

   a. There should be a minimum clearance between the walls of a baffle of 4'-0".

   b. Simple handrails between 2'-8" and 3'-0" high should be mounted on the walls of the baffle to aid semi-ambulant people in moving through it.

   c. Handrails should be able to support 250 lbs.

# Fences

Fencing is one element in the exterior environment that has specifically been used as a barrier. For this reason, the subject matter below will only deal with safety factors involved when fencing is used in public areas.

When using fencing, the designer should be aware of the following conditions:

1. Unless specifically designed for security purposes, fencing should not present any unnecessarily dangerous situations for children or other people who might be tempted to climb over or on it.

2. Posts should be sunk adequately into the ground so that the fence does not collapse during high winds or with the weight of a climber.

3. The fence fabric should be well secured to all posts for similar reasons.

4. Fencing should be free of any projections or appendages which might prove dangerous to people on an adjacent walkway, playing field, etc.

# Railings

1. Railings should be placed between 2'-6" to 3'-0" off the ground.

2. Where safety is an important concern, there should be at least 2 parallel bars that occur below the top rail. These should be no further apart than 1'-0". Additional security may be had with the application of a structural screen to the railing.

3. A 2" to 3" high curb placed 4" in front of a railing will prevent the footrest of a wheelchair or other wheeled vehicle from striking the vertical supports of the railing as it moves adjacent to it.

4. Railings should be designed to support a minimum of 250 lbs. and should be kept securely fastened at all times.

5. **Chains:**

   a. Chains intended for use as protective safety barriers should be avoided. Their inher-

## Rail Spacing

■ Spacing between vertical and horizontal members should avoid 5" to 7" openings, since children's heads are easily caught between members.

## Chain Barriers

2'-8" min. ht. at sag point

■ Chains can be extremely hazardous to pedestrians, bicyclists, and motorcyclists since they are extremely difficult to see, especially when below the 2'-8" level.
■ reflectorized devices should be placed on chains to warn nighttime travellers of their presence.

■ provide additional protection where heights are great or where children might crawl through.

■ 2"-3" curb prevents objects from rolling under railing.

# General Considerations for Railings

ent flexibility does not lend itself well to either stopping pedestrian traffic or to giving solid support to someone needing it. Their best use is to act as an inexpensive vehicular barrier. Unless they are adequetely identified, they may present an extreme hazard to bicyclists, motorcyclists, and the partially sighted or blind.

b. When used as vehicle barriers, chains should be suspended between sturdy, well-anchored supports in such a way that at the lowest, or most slack point, the chain is a minimum of 2'-8" above the ground.

c. The chain should be well marked with reflectorized devices so that it can be easily seen at night.

■ All exposed fastening devices and fabric edges should be rounded off or "knuckled" to prevent cuts and abrasions.

■ Additional space should be provided here to retain objects from falling onto lower level. Set back also gives many people a greater sense of security where heights are great.

65

# Waiting Areas, Drop-off Zones, and Parking

## Considerations for Waiting Areas

**Bus Stop Shelters**
a.) allow views of oncoming busses
b.) bus route information
c.) shelter from elements
d.) 5 footcandle lighting
e.) transparent sides for visability & safety.
f.) provide space for wheelchairs.

■ allow space for strollers, canes, wheelchairs, etc.

■ space large enough for people in groups.

■ shaded sitting provides greater comfort for extended wait.

Transportation mode change areas such as parking lots, bus stops, train stations, and air-line terminals tend to be confusing and difficult to negotiate due to their size, the large amounts of traffic usually associated with them, and the necessity to change grade levels. Generally, if access through these areas is made simple for wheelchair dependent people, or for people pushing strollers or dollies, then access is made easier for all people. The three major site areas concerned with mode change are waiting areas, drop-off zones, and parking facilities.

## Waiting Areas

Waiting areas for mass transit are perhaps the most common of all exterior waiting areas. Due to the large amount of time spent waiting for buses and trains, it is important that these areas be physically accommodating for all people.

When designing exterior waiting areas, the following items should be considered:

1. The waiting area should be large enough to comfortably accommodate the average number of people normally using it.

2. Seating should be provided for the average number of daily users, with space also allotted to park wheelchairs, strollers, and other wheeled vehicles.

3. Where possible, an overhead shelter or canopy should be used to minimize the effects of the weather. Care should be taken to locate vertical support posts out of the paths of pedestrians either using or passing near the shelter. If the shelter is enclosed, adequate space must be allotted for easy movement into and through it.

4. Make sure that waiting area designs allow passengers to see approaching vehicles before they arrive at the stop. This courtesy allows all passengers time to adequately prepare themselves for boarding and as a result, shorten loading times for vehicles and reduce embar-

rassing situations for handicapped individuals.

5. Loading areas should be designed so that circulation from the waiting area is uncomplicated and over paved surfaces. The loading area itself should not have a curb that must be climbed. If a curb cannot be avoided, a 1:6 ramp will be necessary.

## Drop-off Zones

Drop-off zones are beneficial for letting off and picking up people who are laden with packages, have children in strollers, or are physically restricted in some way.

The designer should consider the following items:

1. The width of the drop-off zone should be a minimum of 12'-0" wide to allow the car doors to be fully opened for ease of access.

2. Length of the zone should accommodate at least 2 cars, allowing 25'-0" for each, and should have gradual access to the main road.

3. Where the zone is at the same grade as the adjacent walk, bollards or some other suitable device should be used to separate the two functions. Where a curb exists and cannot be removed, one small 1:6 ramp per car should be provided to make the grade change.

4. Signage should be provided to identify the drop-off zone and limit its defined use to a "pick-up — drop off" function.

5. For recommended lighting levels, see "Lighting. Considerations."

6. **Bollards:**
   a. Bollards are useful as traffic control devices as they allow for pedestrian access

# Bus Stops & Waiting Areas

- 5' MIN. ADDITIONAL PAVING IS RECOMMENDED TO ELIMINATE CONGESTION OF THROUGH PEDESTRIAN TRAFFIC ON WALK.

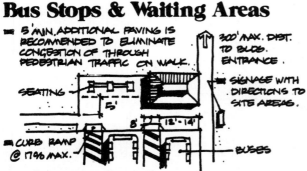

- 300' MAX. DIST. TO BLDG. ENTRANCE.
- SIGNAGE WITH DIRECTIONS TO SITE AREAS.
- SEATING
- CURB RAMP @ 17% MAX.
- BUSES
- BUS STALLS TYPICALLY 12'/14' × 30'/40'.
- PEDESTRIAN AISLES BETWEEN BUSES ALLOW ACCESS FOR LOADING AND UNLOADING.

## 1. Perpendicular Stalls

- 5' MIN. ADDITIONAL PAVING

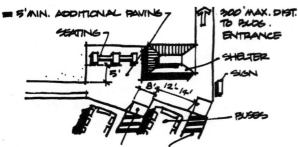

- 300' MAX. DIST. TO BLDG. ENTRANCE
- SEATING
- SHELTER
- SIGN
- BUSES
- CURB RAMPS @ 17% MAX TO ALLOW WHEELED VEHICLES ACCESS BETWEEN BUSES.
- PEDESTRIAN AISLES PAINTED BETWEEN BUSES.

## 2. Angled Stalls

- 5' MIN. ADDITIONAL PAVING

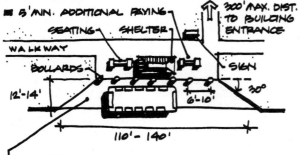

- 300' MAX. DIST. TO BUILDING ENTRANCE
- SEATING
- SHELTER
- WALK WAY
- BOLLARDS
- SIGN
- 30°
- 12'-14'
- 6'-10'
- 110' - 140'
- PULL-OFF RAMPED UP TO MEET WAITING AREA PAVEMENT. BOLLARDS KEEP VEHICLES OUT OF PEDESTRIAN AREAS.

## 3. Parallel Drop-Offs

- CURB CUTS PROVIDED TO ALLOW CURB-FREE ACCESS TO PEDESTRIAN AISLES BETWEEN BUSES.

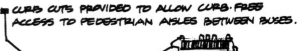

- 6" CURB
- PEDESTRIAN AISLES BETWEEN BUSES ALLOW ACCESS FOR LOADING AND UNLOADING.

## 4. Level-Stalls with Curbs

- RAMPED STALLS ALLOW CURB-FREE ACCESS TO BUSES.

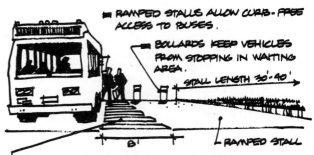

- BOLLARDS KEEP VEHICLES FROM STOPPING IN WAITING AREA.
- STALL LENGTH 30'-40'
- 8'
- RAMPED STALL
- PAINTED AISLES BETWEEN VEHICLES.

## 5. Ramped Stalls

- 70'-100'    30'-40'

- STOPS LOCATED AT CORNERS REQUIRE BAYS OF 70'-100' FOR SINGLE BUSES; 30'-50' FOR EACH ADDITIONAL BUS.

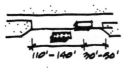

- 110'-140'    30'-50'

- STOPS LOCATED AT MID-BLOCK AREAS WILL REQUIRE BAYS OF 110'-140' FOR SINGLE BUSES; 30'-50' FOR EACH ADDITIONAL BUS.

- MEASUREMENTS ASSUME LENGTH OF BUS TO BE 30'-40' TYPICAL.

## 6. Lengths for Parallel Drop-Offs

# Bus Stop Considerations

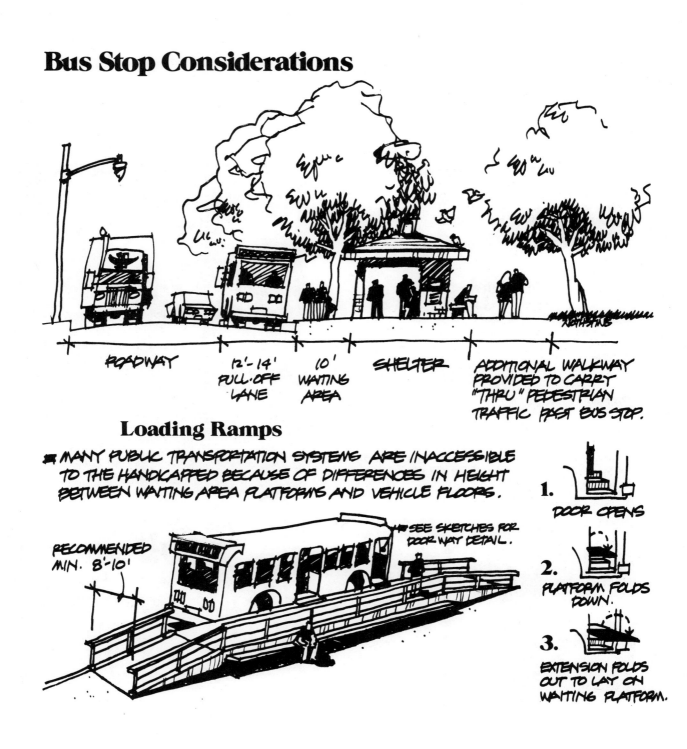

ROADWAY    12'-14' PULL-OFF LANE    10' WAITING AREA    SHELTER    ADDITIONAL WALKWAY PROVIDED TO CARRY "THRU" PEDESTRIAN TRAFFIC PAST BUS STOP.

## Loading Ramps

❋ MANY PUBLIC TRANSPORTATION SYSTEMS ARE INACCESSIBLE TO THE HANDICAPPED BECAUSE OF DIFFERENCES IN HEIGHT BETWEEN WAITING AREA PLATFORMS AND VEHICLE FLOORS.

RECOMMENDED MIN. 8'-10'

☞ SEE SKETCHES FOR DOOR WAY DETAIL.

**1.** DOOR OPENS

**2.** PLATFORM FOLDS DOWN.

**3.** EXTENSION FOLDS OUT TO LAY ON WAITING PLATFORM.

## Pedestrian Considerations at Bus Stops

■ 6' MIN. RECOMMENDED WALK TO CARRY "THRU" PEDESTRIANS.

GENERAL PEDESTRIAN WAITING AREA.

■ BUS STOPS ALONG HEAVILY TRAVELLED WALKS SHOULD PROVIDE ADEQUATE PAVEMENT TO ALLOW "THRU" PEDESTRIAN TRAFFIC TO AVOID CONGESTED WAITING AREAS.

# Drop-Off Areas

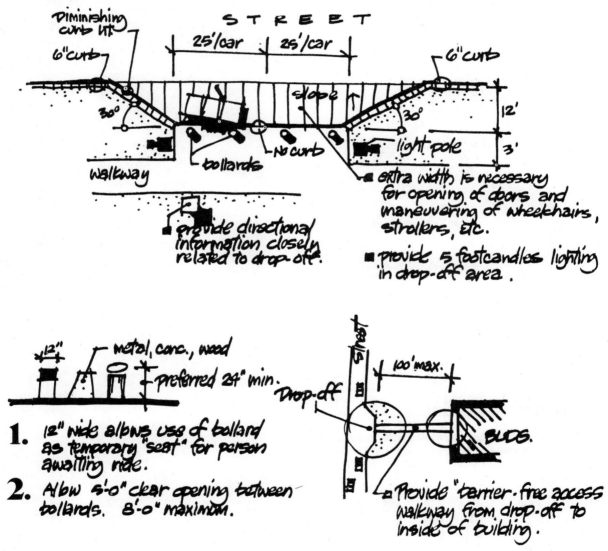

S T R E E T

Diminishing curb ht.

6" curb

25'/car | 25'/car

30°

slope ↑

6" curb

12'

3'

No curb

light pole

walkway

bollards

■ extra width is necessary for opening of doors and maneuvering of wheelchairs, strollers, etc.

provide directional information closely related to drop-off.

■ provide 5 footcandles lighting in drop-off area.

12"

metal, conc., wood

preferred 24" min.

1. 12" wide allows use of bollard as temporary "seat" for person awaiting ride.
2. Allow 5'-0" clear opening between bollards. 8'-0" maximum.

Street

100' max.

Drop-off

BLDG.

■ Provide "barrier-free access walkway from drop-off to inside of building.

## Bollards                    ## Distance to Building

71

## Drop·Off Zones

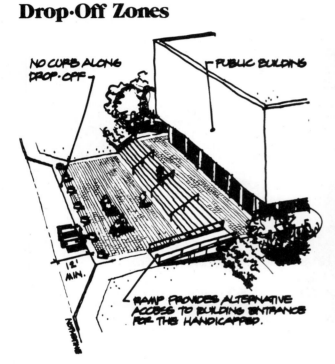

NO CURB ALONG DROP·OFF

PUBLIC BUILDING

12' MIN.

RAMP PROVIDES ALTERNATIVE ACCESS TO BUILDING ENTRANCE FOR THE HANDICAPPED.

## Bollards

12' MIN.

BOLLARDS ARE USED TO SEPARATE VEHICULAR AND PEDESTRIAN TRAFFIC WHERE GRADE·FREE ACCESS IS DESIRABLE ACROSS EXISTING CURBS.

24" MIN.

BOLLARDS CAN BE OBTAINED OR MANUFACTURED FROM A WIDE VARIETY OF MATERIALS. LIGHTING ELEMENTS CAN BE INCORPORATED INTO BOLLARDS TO ADD ADDITIONAL DESIGN INTEREST AND NIGHT·TIME SAFETY.

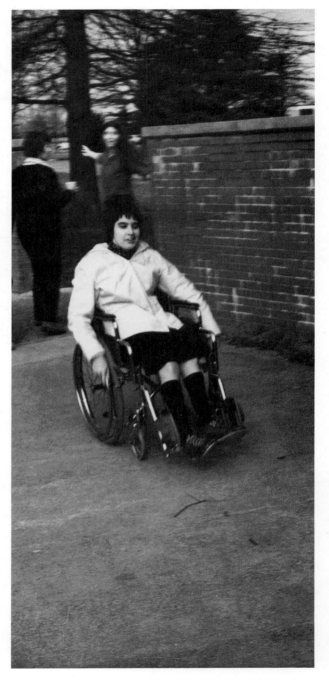

while halting vehicular access. They should be spaced a minimum of 3'-0" apart to allow a wheelchair to pass.

b. Bollards can be useful for seats if they are at least 12" wide, and between 18" to 24" high.

c. Bollards should be painted in a contrasting color to the paving they rest on and should be well illuminated at night to minimize the risk of a person inadvertently walking into them.

# Parking

1. Parking spaces of greater width than normal are necessary for people who are disabled and use mechanical aids such as wheelchairs, crutches, and walkers. For example, a person who is chairbound must have a wider aisle in which to set up his wheelchair.

2. A minimum of two spaces per parking lot should be designed for use by physically restricted people, or at least one space per 20 cars, whichever is greater.

3. These spaces should be placed as close as possible to a major entrance of a building or function, preferably no more than 100'-0" away.

4. For recommended lighting levels, see "Lighting Considerations."

5. **Parallel Parking:**
Parallel parking spaces should be placed adjacent to a walk system so that access from the car to the destination is over a hard surface. Such spaces should be made 12'-0" wide, 24'-0" long and should either have a 1:6 ramp up to the walk, or should be separated from it by bollards or some other device if the road level is at the same elevation as the walk. These areas should be designated as special

parking since they may otherwise appear to be a drop-off zone.

6. **90 Degree and Angled Parking:**
a. Spaces designed for use by disabled people functioning with large mechanical aids as described above, should be 9'-0" wide as a minimum. In addition to the 9'-0", a 3'-6" to 4'-0" wide aisle between cars should be provided for access alongside the vehicle. It is important that there be plenty of room to open the car door entirely, and in the case of a dependent chairbound person, that there be room for friends or attendants to assist him out of the car, into his chair, and away from the car.

b. The 9'-0" wide standard space width for a parking stall, with no aisle between spaces, does not drastically hinder semi-ambulant people with minor impairments, but an 8'-0" width, unless used exclusively for attendant parking, is too narrow and should be avoided.

c. A 4'-0" minimum clear aisle width should be provided between rows of cars parked end to end. The overhang of the automobile should be taken into account so that the island strip is wide enough to leave a 4'-0" clear aisle when the stalls are filled. A strip 8'-0" wide is a recommended minimum for an on-grade aisle, and 10'-0" is a recommended minimum where the aisle is raised 6" above the parking level.

d. If the aisle between rows of cars is not at the same grade level as the cars, then ramps must be provided to mount the curbs. A 1:6 (17%) ramp is suitable for such a short distance.

e. Economically, the installation of an on-grade 4'-0" wide pathway is less expensive than a raised walk. Precast car stops to delineate the passage can be used provided that a 4'-0" wide space between the ends of stops is maintained to allow access to the main passageway.

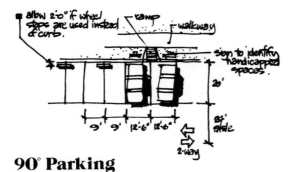

**90° Parking**

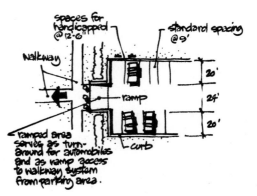

**Parking Using End-Lot Access**

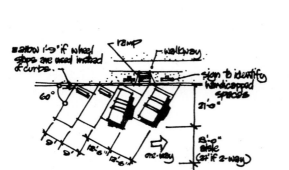

**60° Parking**

**Cross-Slope in Parking Areas**

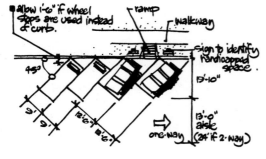

**45° Parking**

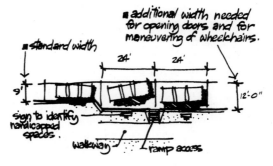

**Parallel Parking**

f. Parking spaces specifically designed for restricted individuals should be set aside and properly identified through the use of signage so that the spaces are not used indiscriminately by people not needing them.

7. Special elevated platforms, or mechanical lifts attached to vehicles must be provided to facilitate boarding and disembarkment by wheelchair bound people from mass transit vehicles.

area beneath bumper overhang may not grow grass. consider low planting or stone. allow 3'-0"

standard 9'-10' spaces

4'-0" aisle

provide ramp access where curbs are present. max. gradient 1:6 (17%)

aisle through parking must be clearly delineated to avoid car parking.

# Aisle Spaces for Pedestrians

# Parking Considerations

- PLANT MATERIAL TO PROVIDE PROTECTION FROM GLARE AND HEAT. AVOID THOSE MATERIALS WHICH DROP EXCESSIVE DEBRIS.

- LIGHTING PROVIDED FOR NIGHT USE @ MINIMUM OF 1 AVG. FOOTCANDLE THROUGHOUT LOT.

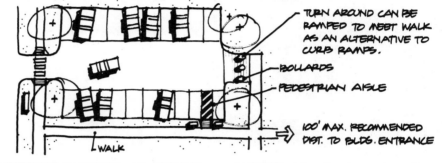

TURN AROUND CAN BE RAMPED TO MEET WALK AS AN ALTERNATIVE TO CURB RAMPS.

BOLLARDS

PEDESTRIAN AISLE

100' MAX. RECOMMENDED DIST. TO BLDG. ENTRANCE

WALK

- ENTRANCE TO PARKING AREA INDICATED WITH SIGNAGE DIRECTING HANDICAPPED TO APPROPRIATE STALLS.

- LOCATE HANDICAP STALLS NEAREST TO BLDG. ENTRANCE.

- PROVIDE CURB RAMP @ 17% MAX. WHERE CURB EXISTS.

## 1. General Layout

- 4' PEDESTRIAN AISLE LOCATED BETWEEN EVERY OTHER SPACE AS SHOWN ABOVE.

- CAR STALLS AT 8' MIN., PREF. 9'-10'.

- ALLOW 3' FOR BUMPER OVERHANG ON CARS WHEN WALK IS ADJACENT TO STALLS.

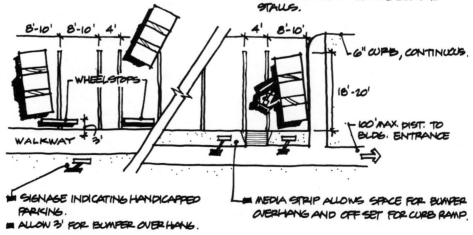

8'-10'  8'-10'  4'

WHEELSTOPS

WALKWAY  3'

4'  8'-10'

6" CURB, CONTINUOUS.

18'-20'

100' MAX. DIST. TO BLDG. ENTRANCE

- SIGNAGE INDICATING HANDICAPPED PARKING.
- ALLOW 3' FOR BUMPER OVERHANG.

- MEDIA STRIP ALLOWS SPACE FOR BUMPER OVERHANG AND OFFSET FOR CURB RAMP.

## 2. Plan View Detail

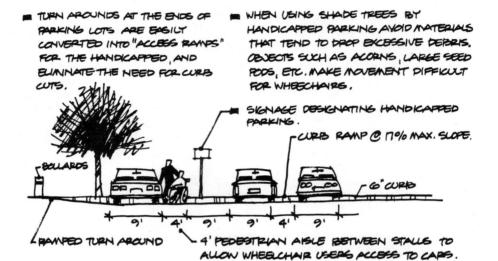

- TURN AROUNDS AT THE ENDS OF PARKING LOTS ARE EASILY CONVERTED INTO "ACCESS RAMPS" FOR THE HANDICAPPED, AND ELIMINATE THE NEED FOR CURB CUTS.

- WHEN USING SHADE TREES BY HANDICAPPED PARKING AVOID MATERIALS THAT TEND TO DROP EXCESSIVE DEBRIS. OBJECTS SUCH AS ACORNS, LARGE SEED PODS, ETC. MAKE MOVEMENT DIFFICULT FOR WHEELCHAIRS.

SIGNAGE DESIGNATING HANDICAPPED PARKING.

CURB RAMP @ 17% MAX. SLOPE.

6" CURB

BOLLARDS

RAMPED TURN AROUND

4' PEDESTRIAN AISLE BETWEEN STALLS TO ALLOW WHEELCHAIR USERS ACCESS TO CARS.

## 3. Cross-Section

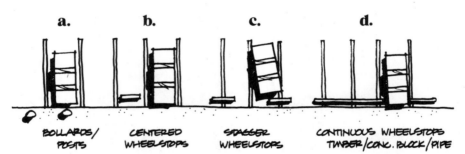

**a.** BOLLARDS/ POSTS

**b.** CENTERED WHEELSTOPS

**c.** STAGGER WHEELSTOPS

**d.** CONTINUOUS WHEELSTOPS TIMBER/CONC. BLOCK/PIPE

- WHEELSTOPS ALLOW CURB-FREE ACCESS TO AND FROM LOT.

- HANDICAPPED ACCESS IS EASILY HANDLED, PROVIDING AISLE SPACE IS PROVIDED.

- WHEELSTOPS SHOULD CONTRAST WITH COLOR OF PAVEMENT SO THAT THEY ARE EASILY NOTICED BY MOTORISTS AND PEDESTRIANS.

- CONTINUOUS WHEELSTOPS ARE NOT RECOMMENDED:

PEDESTRIANS ARE EASILY TRIPPED BY RAISED STOP.

ACCESS IS OFTEN DIFFICULT FOR THE HANDICAPPED.

## 4. Curb-Free Parking

# Parking for the Handicapped

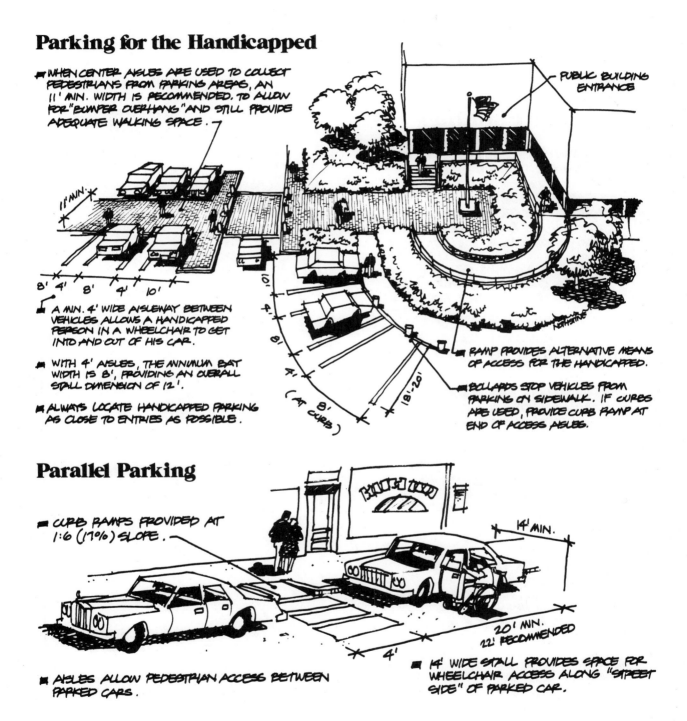

■ WHEN CENTER AISLES ARE USED TO COLLECT PEDESTRIANS FROM PARKING AREAS, AN 11' MIN. WIDTH IS RECOMMENDED. TO ALLOW FOR "BUMPER OVERHANG" AND STILL PROVIDE ADEQUATE WALKING SPACE.

PUBLIC BUILDING ENTRANCE

11' MIN.

8'  4'  8'  4'  10'

■ A MIN. 4' WIDE AISLEWAY BETWEEN VEHICLES ALLOWS A HANDICAPPED PERSON IN A WHEELCHAIR TO GET INTO AND OUT OF HIS CAR.

■ WITH 4' AISLES, THE MINIMUM BAY WIDTH IS 8', PROVIDING AN OVERALL STALL DIMENSION OF 12'.

■ ALWAYS LOCATE HANDICAPPED PARKING AS CLOSE TO ENTRIES AS POSSIBLE.

10'
4'
8'
4'
(AT CURB)

18'-20'

■ RAMP PROVIDES ALTERNATIVE MEANS OF ACCESS FOR THE HANDICAPPED.

■ BOLLARDS STOP VEHICLES FROM PARKING ON SIDEWALK. IF CURBS ARE USED, PROVIDE CURB RAMP AT END OF ACCESS AISLES.

# Parallel Parking

■ CURB RAMPS PROVIDED AT 1:6 (17%) SLOPE.

14' MIN.

4'

20' MIN.
22' RECOMMENDED

■ AISLES ALLOW PEDESTRIAN ACCESS BETWEEN PARKED CARS.

■ 14' WIDE STALL PROVIDES SPACE FOR WHEELCHAIR ACCESS ALONG "STREET SIDE" OF PARKED CAR.

# Vegetation Considerations

## Outdoor Plantings

- OVERHEAD MATERIALS SHOULD BE CHOSEN FOR THEIR PARTICULAR CHARACTERISTICS. AVOID MATERIALS THAT HAVE TENDENCIES TOWARDS DROPPING EXCESSIVE DEBRIS, DROOPING OR BREAKING UNDER HEAVY SNOW LOADS, OR WINDS, ETC.

- MAINTAIN A MINIMUM OF 8'-6" VERTICAL CLEARANCE OVER WALKS, BIKEWAYS, SITTING AREAS, ETC.

- IMPROPER LOCATION OR POOR MAINTENANCE CAN QUICKLY LEAD TO A REDUCTION OF THE EFFICIENCY OF LIGHTING SYSTEMS.

- AVOID PLACING HAZARDOUS OR NUISANCE MATERIALS ADJACENT TO WALKWAY OR SITTING AREAS.

- PLANT MATERIALS MAY AFFECT THE MELTING OF ICE AND SNOW FROM WALKWAYS AND STAIRS. CONSIDER THEIR MATURE SHADOW PATTERNS DURING WINTER MONTHS BEFORE DECIDING ON THEIR FINAL LOCATIONS.

- MANY TREES WITH SHALLOW OR SURFACE ROOT SYSTEMS WILL HEAVE OR BREAK UP WALKWAY SURFACES. USE CAUTION WHEN CHOOSING THESE VARIETIES AND THEIR SUBSEQUENT LOCATIONS.

- AVOID PLACING MATERIALS OVER OR NEAR UNDERGROUND UTILITIES. IF THEY HAVE ROOT SYSTEMS THAT CHARACTERISTICALLY CAUSE DAMAGE TO PIPELINES, CABLES, SEWERS, ETC.

- CREEPING GROUND COVERS, VINES AND OTHER INVASIVE MATERIALS CAN BE TROUBLESOME IF NOT CONTAINED- KEEP THEM OFF BUILDINGS, WALKWAYS, STEPS, RAMPS, SIGNS, AND LIGHTING FIXTURES.

# Fundamentals

Listing the mechanics for introducing plant materials in public areas is beyond the scope of this book. However, there are some very basic considerations worth mentioning concerning placement, choice, and maintenance that should be observed by the designer.

1. Potentially dangerous plants such as those having large thorns or those with poisonous fruit should not be placed immediately adjacent to major walks where they may present a hazard. This is not to say that such plant material should not be used near heavily travelled areas, but only that it should be used with discretion. (See chart next page)

2. Proper maintenance of plant material is necessary to assure that dangerous situations do not arise. Seed pods, berries or fruit that may produce a slippery surface should be removed. Branches that overhang walks should be pruned to a height of 8'-6" above the ground to prevent eye or face injuries.

3. In areas where snow is a common winter occurrence careful consideration should be given to the type and location of plants which will be placed along public thoroughfares because:

   a. Species which have a tendency to break under ice and snow loads should be kept away from heavily trafficked areas.

   b. "Snow droop" can cause branches to bend below a safe level above walkways and streets. It should be determined whether or not these branches present a hazard so that they may be pruned accordingly.

4. Plant material is useful for providing shelter from the sun, and to an extent, from the wind.

5. Plant materials can be used effectively as barriers in controlling the movements of people through public spaces or in keeping them away from hazardous areas.

6. Avoid placement of planting materials where their shadows might prevent the effective melting of ice and snow by the sun.

# Hazard/Nuisance | Species | Comments

| Hazard/Nuisance | Species | Comments |
|---|---|---|
| 1. POISONOUS PLANTS: | HOLLY, YEW, PRIVET, LAUREL, RHODODENDRON. | CHILDREN MAY BE TEMPTED TO SAMPLE BRIGHT COLORED BERRIES OR LEAVES. |
| 2. DEBRIS: | | |
| a. FRUITS & NUTS: | CRABAPPLE, PLUM, CHERRY, OAK, CHESTNUT, HICKORY, WALNUT. | LONG, STRAP-LIKE PODS, BERRIES, CONES, & NUTS, CAN BE SLIPPERY OR DIFFICULT TO WALK ON. THEY ARE EASILY TRACKED INTO BUILDINGS, AND CAN STAIN CLOTHING IF SAT UPON. |
| b. CONES: | PINES, SPRUCE, FIR, LARCH, HEMLOCK. | CONES, WHILE HAVING MANY DECORATIVE USES CAN CAUSE PROBLEMS FOR PEDESTRIANS AND SMALL-WHEELED VEHICLES WHEN THEY FALL ON WALKWAY SURFACES. |
| c. SEED PODS: | SWEETGUM, SYCAMORE, LONDON PLANETREE, HONEY LOCUST MAPLE. | PODS CREATE UNSURE FOOTING FOR PEDESTRIANS AND HINDER THE MOVEMENTS OF SMALL-WHEELED VEHICLES. |
| d. BRANCH BREAKAGE: | BIRCH, SILVER MAPLE, BOX-ELDER, HORSE CHESTNUT, POPLAR, WILLOW, TULIPTREE, ELM. | BRANCH DEBRIS IS DIFFICULT TO WALK ON OR PUSH SMALL-WHEELED VEHICLES OVER. LARGE BRANCHES CAN CAUSE EXTENSIVE DAMAGE TO ITEMS ON WHICH THEY MIGHT HAPPEN TO FALL SUCH AS CARS, SMALL WOOD FRAME STRUCTURES, ETC. |
| 3. DROOPING BRANCHES: | BIRCH, WILLOW, PIN OAK, BEECH, MAGNOLIA. | BRANCHES CAN DROP BELOW MINIMUM CLEARANCES ON WALKWAYS OR STREETS CAUSING FACIAL OR EYE INJURIES TO PEDESTRIANS OR HAZARDS FOR MOTORISTS. |
| 4. SHALLOW ROOTS: | WILLOW, RED MAPLE, SILVER MAPLE, BEECH, COTTONWOOD, POPLAR VARIETIES | SURFACE ROOT SYSTEMS CAN CAUSE WALKS TO HEAVE AND BREAK APART WHICH IN TURN CAN CAUSE PEDESTRIANS TO TRIP AND FALL. UNEVEN OR BROKEN SURFACES CAN BE EXTREMELY DIFFICULT TO PUSH SMALL-WHEELED VEHICLES OVER. |
| 5. ODOR: | SIEBOLD VIBURNUM, FEMALE GINKGO | FOUL SMELLING ODORS NOT ONLY DETRACT FROM AN AREA'S AESTHETIC APPEAL BUT TEND TO MAKE SOME PEOPLE NAUSEOUS. |
| 6. THORNS & SPIKES: | BARBERRY, QUINCE, HAWTHORNE, LOCUST, HOLLY, ROSE VARIETIES PRIVET | PLANTS WITH THORNS OR SPIKES CAN BE EXTREMELY PAINFUL TO BRUSH AGAINST OR FALL INTO. LEAVES, TWIGS, OR BRANCHES WHICH FALL TO THE GROUND ARE ALSO HAZARDOUS FOR PEOPLE IN BAREFEET OR LIGHT FOOTWARE. |
| 7. INSECTS & PESTS: | FRUIT TREES (CRABAPPLE, CHERRY PLUM, ETC.) MOUNTAIN LAUREL | BECAUSE OF THE SEVERE REACTION CERTAIN PEOPLE HAVE TO MANY INSECT BITES AND STINGS, THE LOCATION OF PLANT MATERIALS WHICH ATTRACT THESE PESTS ARE NOT RECOMMENDED FOR AREAS ADJACENT TO WALKS OR SITTING AREAS. |

# Lighting Considerations

## Lumen:

A unit for measuring the amount of light energy given off by a light source (bulb).

## Footcandle:

A unit for measuring the amount of illumination on a surface.

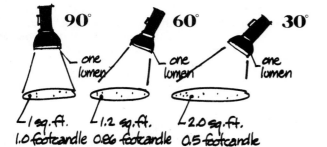

90°  one lumen  └ 1 sq.ft.  1.0 footcandle

60°  one lumen  └ 1.2 sq.ft.  0.86 footcandle

30°  one lumen  └ 2.0 sq.ft.  0.5 footcandle

The amount of useable light from a given source will vary according to the angle of incidence and the distance to the illuminated surface.

## Lateral Light Distribution

■ Light patterns can be varied according to the needs of a particular situation. Choose the proper pattern and fixture for your specific requirements.

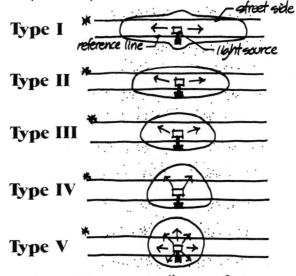

Type I  * ← street side, reference line, light source

Type II

Type III

Type IV

Type V

\* IES standard light pattern classifications.

## Light Intensity

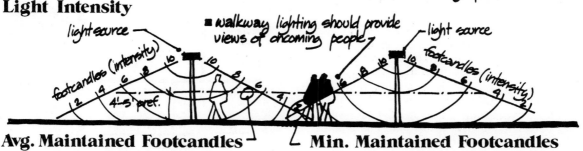

light source · walkway lighting should provide views of oncoming people · light source

footcandles (intensity)  10 8 6 4 2

4'-5' pref.

footcandles (intensity)  10 8 6 4 2

## Avg. Maintained Footcandles

* Measured at average point of illumination between brightest area and darkest areas. Can be measured at ground surface or at 4'-5' above walkway surface.

## Min. Maintained Footcandles

* Measured on ground surface at point of least illumination.

Note: Where intensity curves overlap, the resulting intensity is the combined total of the two ratings.

# Purpose and Application

The purpose of site lighting is basically twofold: (1) to illuminate, and (2) to provide security. Lighting should be provided in areas that receive heavy pedestrian or vehicular use and in areas that are dangerous if unlit, such as stairs and ramps, intersections or abrupt changes in grade. Likewise, areas that have high crime rates should be well lit in order that people traveling at night may feel personally secure from attack.

The phrase "well lit" has a wider meaning than simply higher light levels. Unless light is placed where it is really the most useful, the expense of increasing footcandle levels is wasted. An area may need only the addition of a few more lights to correct its problems, not an increase in light levels from fixtures that are too few, or poorly located.

When considering the installation or renovation of lighting systems, the designer should be aware of the following considerations:

1. Overhead lamps have the advantage over low-level fixtures of providing better economy and more even light distribution.

2. Fixtures should be placed so that light patterns overlap at a height of 7'-0", which is sufficiently high to vertically illuminate a person's body. This is a particularly important consideration now that lighting fixture manufacturers are designing luminaires with highly controlled light patterns.

3. At hazardous locations such as changes of grade, lower level supplemental lighting or additional overhead units should be used.

4. Where low-level lighting (below 5'-0") is used, fixtures should be placed in such a way that they do not produce glare. Most eye levels occur between 3'-8" (for wheelchair users) and 6'-0" for standing adults.

5. Posts and standards along thoroughfares should be placed so that they do not present hazards to pedestrians or vehicles.

6. A minor consideration is the use of shatterproof coverings on low-level lighting where there is the chance of breakage from vandalism or mishaps from people playing frisbee, football, baseball, etc. The absence of any resulting broken material will reduce otherwise potential hazards.

7. **Peripheral Lighting:**
   When walkway lighting is provided primarily by low fixtures, there should be sufficient peripheral lighting to illuminate the immediate surroundings. Peripheral lighting provides for a better feeling of security for an individual since he can see into his surroundings to determine whether or not passage through an area is safe. Such lighting should be approached from one of two ways:

   a. By lighting the area so that an object or person may be seen directly.

   b. By lighting the area to place an object or person in silhouette.

# IES Tree Pruning Recommendations*

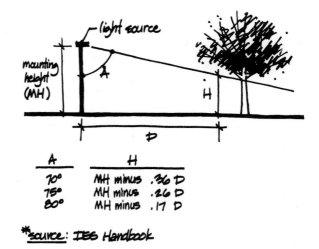

| A | H |
|---|---|
| 70° | MH minus .36 D |
| 75° | MH minus .26 D |
| 80° | MH minus .17 D |

*source: IES Handbook

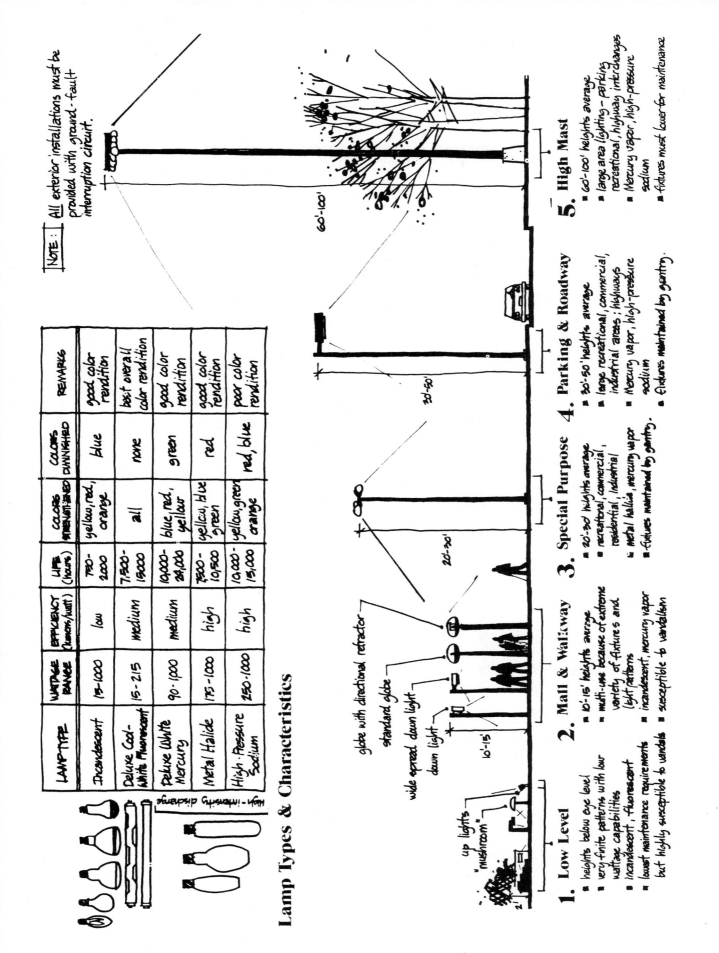

## Lamp Types & Characteristics

| LAMP TYPE | WATTAGE RANGE | EFFICIENCY (lumens/watt) | LIFE (hours) | COLORS STRENGTHENED | COLORS DIMINISHED | REMARKS |
|---|---|---|---|---|---|---|
| Incandescent | 15-1000 | low | 750-1000 | yellow, red, orange | blue | good color rendition |
| Deluxe Cool-White Fluorescent | 15-215 | medium | 7,500-15000 | all | none | best overall color rendition |
| Deluxe White Mercury | 90-1000 | medium | 10,000-24,000 | blue, red, yellow | green | good color rendition |
| Metal Halide | 175-1000 | high | 7500-10500 | yellow, blue green | red | good color rendition |
| High-Pressure Sodium | 250-1000 | high | 10,000-15,000 | yellow, green orange | red, blue | poor color rendition |

high-intensity discharge

NOTE: All exterior installations must be provided with ground-fault interruption circuit.

glass with directional refractor
standard globe
wide spread down light
down light
up lights "mushroom"

### 1. Low Level
- heights below eye level
- very finite patterns with low wattage capabilities
- incandescent, fluorescent
- lowest maintenance requirements but highly susceptible to vandals

### 2. Mall & Walkway
- 10-15' heights average
- multi-use because of extreme variety of fixtures and light patterns
- incandescent, mercury vapor
- susceptible to vandalism

### 3. Special Purpose
- 20-30' heights average
- recreational, commercial, residential, industrial
- metal halide, mercury vapor
- fixtures maintained by gantry.

### 4. Parking & Roadway
- 20-50' heights average
- large recreational, commercial, industrial areas; highways
- Mercury vapor, high-pressure sodium
- fixtures maintained by gantry.

### 5. High Mast
- 60-100' heights average
- large area lighting – parking, recreational, highway interchanges
- Mercury vapor, high-pressure sodium
- fixtures must lower for maintenance

# IES Recommended Lighting Levels

|  |  | Commercial | Industrial | Residential |
|---|---|---|---|---|
| **I.** | **Pedestrian Areas** | | | |
|  | 1. SIDEWALKS | 0.9[+] | 0.6 | 0.2 |
|  | 2. PEDESTRIAN WAYS | 2.0 | 1.0 | 0.5 |
| **II.** | **Roadways** | | | |
|  | 1. FREEWAYS | 0.6 | 0.6 | 0.6 |
|  | 2. MAJOR AND EXPRESSWAYS | 2.0 | 1.4 | 1.0 |
|  | 3. COLLECTORS | 1.2 | 0.9 | 0.6 |
|  | 4. LOCAL | 0.9 | 0.6 | 0.4 |
|  | 5. ALLEYS | 0.6 | 0.4 | 0.2 |
| **III.** | **Parking Areas** | | | |
|  | 1. SELF PARKING | 1.0 | – | – |
|  | 2. ATTENDENT PARKING | 2.0 | – | – |
| **IV.** | **Buildings** | | | |
|  | 1. ENTRANCE, DOORWAY AREAS | 5.0 | – | – |
|  | 2. GENERAL GROUNDS | 1.0 | – | – |

\*SOURCE: IES LIGHTING HANDBOOK, 4th EDITION
ILLUMINATING ENGINEER'S SOCIETY, NEW YORK CITY, NY

[+] VALUES ARE GIVEN IN MIN. AVG. MAINTAINED HORIZONTAL FOOTCANDLES.

# Types of Distribution

(Note: "Distribution" is measured along LRL.)

mounting height (MH)

Short = 3.75 × MH
Medium = 6.0 × MH
Long = 8.0 × MH

---

light source

light pattern

Roadway

■ Transverse Road Line (TRL)
■ Longitudinal Road Line (LRL)

---

Note: degree of cutoff is determined either by:
 a.) Design of fixture housing
 b.) Incorporation of prismatic lens over light source.
 c.) Addition of shield to fixture on "house side".

---

# Cutoff Terminology

(Note: "cutoff" is measured along TRL.)

"house side"

Roadway

TRANSVERSE ROAD LINE (TRL)

1. Cutoff means maximum of 10% of light source lumens falls outside the TRL area.
2. Semi-Cutoff means maximum of 20% of light source lumens falls outside the TRL area.
3. Non-Cutoff means no control limitations.

# Signage Considerations

## Fundamentals

Essentially, signs should perform three functions. They should: (1) Identify a place and indicate whether or not it is accessible to everyone; (2) Indicate warnings where necessary; and (3) Give routing information.

The information given on signs should always be clear and precise. Sign locations should never present unnecessary hazards for pedestrian or vehicular traffic.

1. **Identification and Accessibility:**

   a. Key site-related areas that should be identified by sign posting are:

      1. Traffic signs announcing public rest stops with accessible facilities.
      2. Public lavatories accessible to pedestrians.
      3. Special car parking.
      4. Directional signs for vehicles and pedestrians such as "one way" street signs.
      5. Signs identifying accessible entrances to buildings or facilities.
      6. Informative signs on buildings.

   b. In order that signs be made more useful to everyone, they should be designed to be readable by all people, including the visually handicapped. This can be accomplished in a number of different ways:
      1. Braille strips can be placed along sign edges.
      2. Raised or routed letters are readable by the blind or partially sighted.
      3. Graphic symbols are useful in transmitting messages quickly, but should be avoided as the sole means of imparting information because they can be confusing to the blind.
      4. Signage that will be used by the visually handicapped must be located in a manner that first allows the sign to be recognized and second, allows the sign surface to be touched by the reader's hand.

      5. Signs along walkways or corridors should be set back a minimum of 18" and placed at a height of 4'-0" to 5'-6".

   c. The international symbol for access, the abstract man in a wheelchair, is already in extensive use in this country. It is used to show where special provisions have been made to allow access for restricted people.

2. **Warnings:**
   a. **Textural Paving:**
      Textural paving may be used to warn of imminent hazards such as abrupt changes of grade, stairs, ramps, walk intersections, etc., and the locations of special information. However, the use of textural paving as a warning device for the blind is extremely impractical because of the widely varying nature of walkways in this country. The only effective use for such a system would be in a closed environment such as a school for the blind. Unfortunately, once away from his protected surroundings, a blind person would be vulnerable to a world full of unforewarned hazards.

3. **Routing Information:**
   Where it is critical that people be able to travel quickly and unhindered to their destinations, routing information should be given.

   a. Hospitals, college campuses, institutions, etc., should have posted signs, lines, or arrows painted on walk systems that are accessible to wheeled vehicles, particularly where such path systems are limited in number.

   b. Access to buildings with only one or two entrances that are accessible to wheeled vehicles should be clearly indicated by routing signs.

4. **Readability:**
   The readability of any sign is a function of many items. When designing or choosing the format of a sign, the following things should be considered:

a. Information should be as concise and direct as possible.

b. Lettering styles and graphic symbols should be as bold and simple as possible. Fancy styles become cluttered, are time consuming, and confusing to read.

c. Color schemes of contrasting colors with light images on dark backgrounds make signs both easier to read and more readable from longer distances.

5. **Placement:**
The placement of signs is important because wrongly located, they may present an obstacle or hazard. Unless intended to be read by the blind or the partially sighted, they should be set far enough off a traveled way and/or high enough off the ground so as not to be inadvertently walked into.

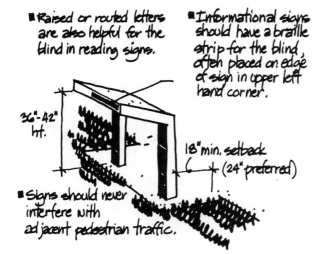

■ Raised or routed letters are also helpful for the blind in reading signs.

■ Informational signs should have a braille strip for the blind, often placed on edge of sign in upper left hand corner.

36"-42" ht.

18" min. setback (24" preferred)

■ Signs should never interfere with adjacent pedestrian traffic.

# Braille on Signs

# Sign Categories & Descriptions

## 1. Directional

Usually included with an arrow; are used for indication of a change in route, or confirmation of a correct direction.

## 2. Informational

Used for overall information for general organization of a series of elements; i.e. campus plan, bus routes, building layout, shopping mall plan, etc.

## 3. Identification

Gives specific location information, identifies specific items; i.e. parking lot "b", building #5, First Aid, etc.

## 4. Regulatory

Gives operational requirements, restrictions, or gives warnings; Usually used for traffic delineation or control; i.e. "Stop" signs, "no parking," "one way," etc.

# Signage Considerations

KEEP SIGNAGE ABOVE 7½-8' HT. WHERE PEDESTRIANS MAY INADVERTANTLY WALK INTO "HEAD HEIGHT" OBJECTS.

7½' MIN.

\* WHERE BICYCLES ARE INVOLVED, SIGNS SHOULD BE KEPT ABOVE AN 8½' HT.

### 1. Vertical Clearances

▪ MIN. SETBACKS OF 24" ARE RECOMMENDED AT CURB AND WALKWAY EDGES TO KEEP PEDESTRIANS FROM ACCIDENTLY WALKING INTO SIGNS OR POSTS.

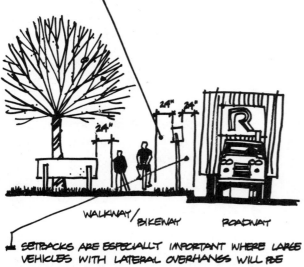

WALKWAY / BIKEWAY     ROADWAY

▪ SETBACKS ARE ESPECIALLY IMPORTANT WHERE LARGE VEHICLES WITH LATERAL OVERHANGS WILL BE OPERATING ALONG NARROW STREETS AND LOADING DOCKS.

### 2. Horizontal Clearances

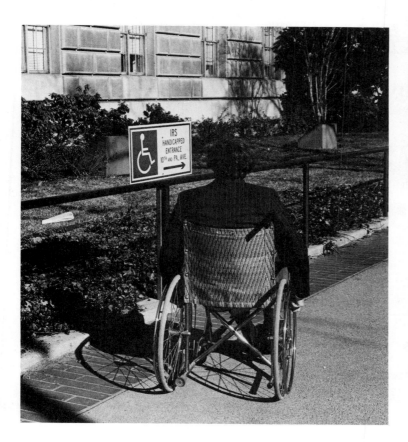

# Design and Location

- When possible, gather signs together into unified systems. Avoid sign clutter in the landscape.

- Combine signs with lighting fixtures to reduce unnecessary posts and to illuminate signs - signage can't be effective in dark areas.

- Low-level informational signs can also illuminate paving below.

- Information signs should be placed at natural gathering spots and included into the design of site furniture.

- Avoid placement of signs where they may conflict with pedestrian traffic.

- Sign location should avoid conflict with door opening or vehicular operation.

- Signs should be placed to allow safe pedestrian clearance, vertically and laterally.

# Signage by N.P.S. & U.S. Forest Service

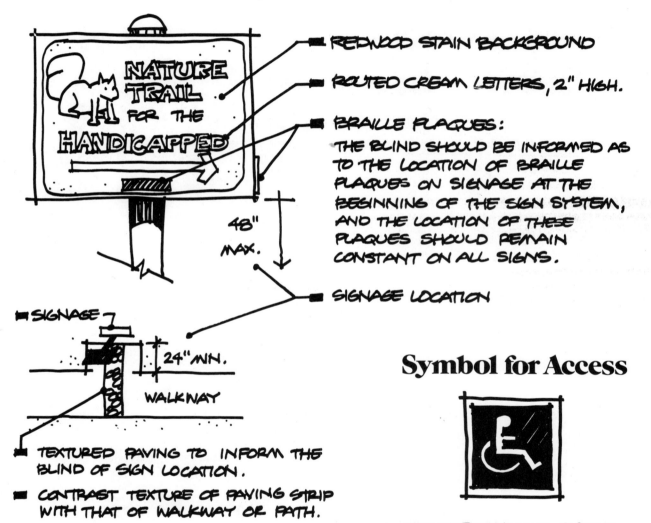

- REDWOOD STAIN BACKGROUND

- ROUTED CREAM LETTERS, 2" HIGH.

- BRAILLE PLAQUES:
  THE BLIND SHOULD BE INFORMED AS TO THE LOCATION OF BRAILLE PLAQUES ON SIGNAGE AT THE BEGINNING OF THE SIGN SYSTEM, AND THE LOCATION OF THESE PLAQUES SHOULD REMAIN CONSTANT ON ALL SIGNS.

- SIGNAGE LOCATION

NATURE TRAIL FOR THE HANDICAPPED

48" MAX.

- SIGNAGE

24" MIN.

WALKWAY

- TEXTURED PAVING TO INFORM THE BLIND OF SIGN LOCATION.

- CONTRAST TEXTURE OF PAVING STRIP WITH THAT OF WALKWAY OR PATH.

- WHEREVER PEDESTRIANS WILL BE STOPPING TO VIEW SIGNS OR EXHIBITS, ADEQUATE OFFSETS SHOULD BE PROVIDED TO ELIMINATE POSSIBLE CONGESTION WITH THROUGH TRAFFIC.

## Symbol for Access

- THE INTERNATIONAL SYMBOL FOR ACCESS IS USED BY BOTH THE N.P.S. & U.S.F.S. TO INDICATE ACCESS FOR THE PHYSICALLY HANDICAPPED PEDESTRIAN.

# Recreation Considerations

## Fundamentals of Play Areas

① <u>ACCESSABLE</u> to all groups.

② <u>SAFETY</u> in choice of elements

③ <u>INTERESTING</u> facilities & apparatus

④ <u>CHALLANGING</u> & <u>INNOVATIVE</u> in the design and layout.

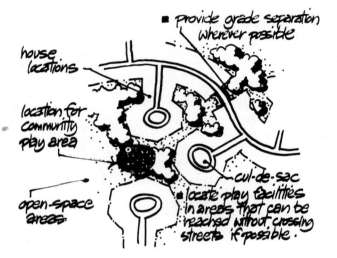

- provide grade separation wherever possible

house locations

location for community play area

open-space areas

cul-de-sac

- locate play facilities in areas that can be reached without crossing streets if possible.

## 1. Community Access to Play

- connect playground paved walkways to community sidewalk system.

- logical organization of play facilities as to type, age, etc.

community sidewalk system

A.

B.

C.

- internal walkways should connect different play elements to each other and allow access to all areas by handicapped.

## 2. Internal Walkways

# Playgrounds

Design segregation of play facilities in regard to varying physical characteristics of children is not, generally speaking, desirable. Playgrounds that are constructed to serve the most diverse segments of society enhance the opportunity of a child's meeting and interacting with a variety of people having differing physical and social characteristics — people with whom he will have to deal in his adult life. In addition to the social aspects, a greater flexibility in the use of a playground is desirable for economic reasons.

In general, play can be grouped into two categories; (1) defined play, and (2) creative play.

Defined play refers to the channeling of play activities into certain prescribed directions. For instance, swings and slides define the child's play within the limits of their function. Although children do many creative things on swings and slides, they are primarily outgrowths of the basic functions of swinging and sliding. On the other hand, creative play primarily arises from the child's imagination. The play element is somewhat amorphic and therefore undefined. A child in a sand area creates sand castles, mountains, rivers, roads, and a plethora of other fantasies straight from his mind. Likewise, free-form sculpture, random climbing blocks, or simply open areas of lawn act as springboards for the imagination.

There seems to be a current trend in which designers heavily specify creative play apparatus for playgrounds, sometimes to the exclusion of defined apparatus. This trend does not well serve children since it does not account for the child who is unable to play creatively.

There are, for instance, thousands of children in this country alone who, handicapped by severe mental and emotional problems, are only able to achieve satisfying play through the use of defined apparatus. Likewise, an imaginative child may quickly lose interest in traditional play equipment whereas a creative apparatus may hold his attention. Therefore, the designer should strive to create a playground that will provide a rich and wide ranging set of both defined and creative experiences.

Just as designers have been designing the environment for the "normal" man, so have playgrounds been designed for the "normal" child. Unfortunately, the child who is physically handicapped usually has restricted motor development, and, as a consequence of his limited movement, does not see the world and himself in the same way as a normal individual would.

By designing play situations in which a disabled child can manipulate his environment as much as possible by himself, regardless of the extent of his disability, the child can have motor experiences comparable to those of normal children. These experiences give a child a broader range of perceptual sophistication and thus a fuller and more normal base for academic growth and self appreciation.

The following criteria are given for consideration in enhancing the use of play facilities both from the standpoint of serving more people and of making the facility safer.

1. A playground should be easily accessible from the adjacent community over hard surface paths, with ramps placed where necessary.

2. Access within the playground should include a system of hard surface paths. Not only does this improve mobility for the handicapped, but can double as a tricycle path.

3. The play area should be reasonably organized in order that a child who is blind may learn how to locate equipment as he enters and moves about the grounds.

4. Apparatus able to accommodate a greater diversity of children does not need to be drastically altered from those now in use. Rather, they must be placed and modified in such a way as to make them both more safe and accessible. Sharp edges, splinters, or poorly designed appurtenances should be eliminated.

5. Playgrounds that are accessible to handicapped children require a certain amount of

The Magruder Environmental Therapy Complex at the Forest Park School in Orlando, Florida was specifically designed to help in developing the motor perception of physically handicapped preschool children. It contains a balance beam, a step progression, a foam pit, slides, rolling hills, mirrors, free standing walls, overhead pull ups and shelters and caves.

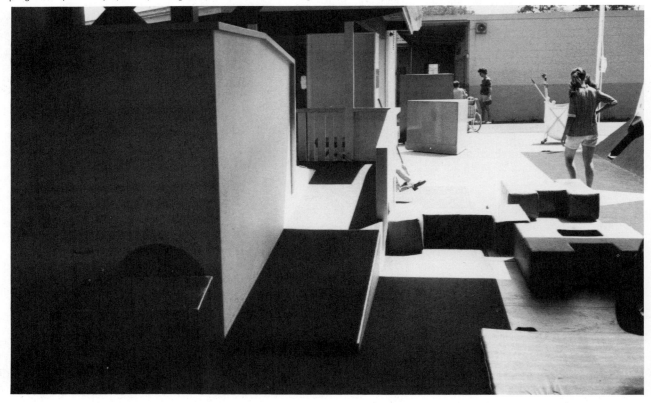

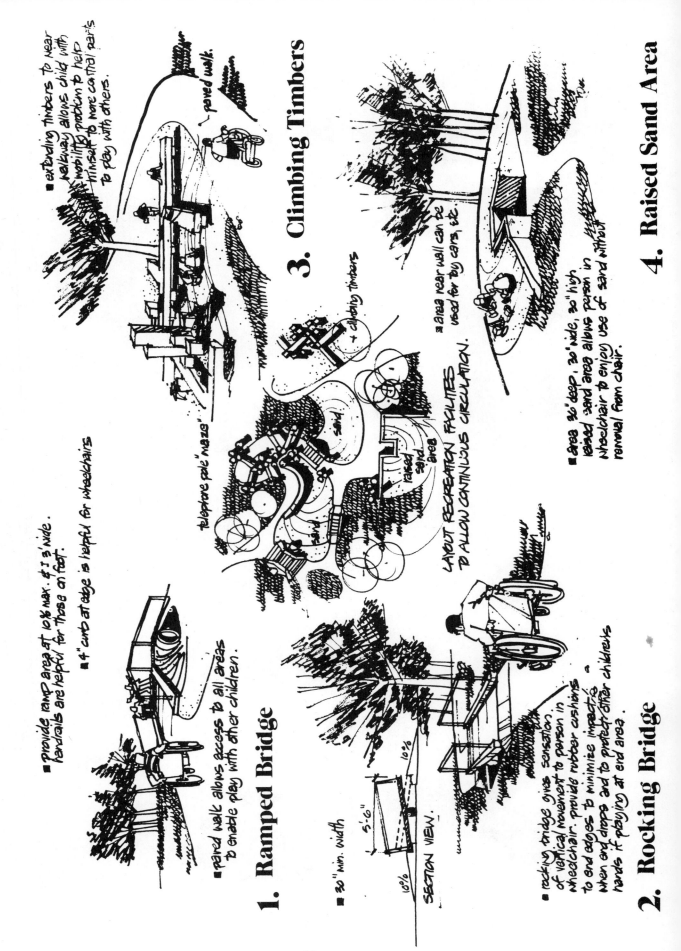

**1. Ramped Bridge**

- extending timbers to near walkway allows child with mobility problem to help himself to more central parts to play with others.
- paved walk.
- paved walk allows access to all areas to enable play with other children.
- provide ramp area at 10% max. & 3' wide. handrails are helpful for those on foot.
- 4" curb at edge is helpful for wheelchairs

**2. Rocking Bridge**

- 30" min. width
- 10%
- 5'-6"
- 10%
- SECTION VIEW.
- rocking bridge gives sensation of vertical movement to person in wheelchair. provide rubber cushions to end edges to minimize impacts when end drops and to protect other children's hands if playing at end area.

**3. Climbing Timbers**

- climbing timbers
- "telephone pole" maze
- sand
- raised sand area
- LAYOUT RECREATION FACILITIES TO ALLOW CONTINUOUS CIRCULATION.

**4. Raised Sand Area**

- area near wall can be used for toy cars, etc.
- area 36" deep, 30" wide, 30" high raised sand area allows person in wheelchair to enjoy use of sand without removal from chair.

98

Grab bars were provided at two levels on the play ramps to allow children of different sizes to use the facilities and equipment.

The Jess Stanton Developmental Playground for Preschool Handicapped Children at the New York University Medical Center was designed to be fully accessible. It contains a bridged treehouse, foam and sand pits, sand and water tables and a hill and circle.

Fold down tables were cut out to allow wheelchair-bound children to use them more fully and easily.

The playground contains sand and water tables designed so that wheelchairs can be pulled up close to the edge of the table to allow the children to reach out on to the table.

# 1. Slides & Climbing Areas

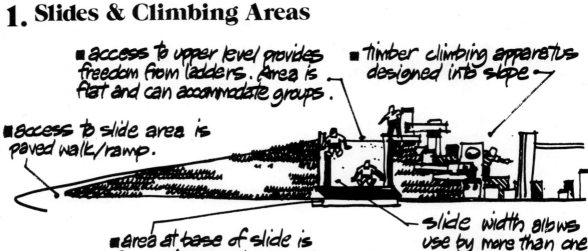

■ access to upper level provides freedom from ladders. Area is flat and can accommodate groups.

■ timber climbing apparatus designed into slope

■ access to slide area is paved walk/ramp.

■ area at base of slide is free-draining and resilient.

■ slide width allows use by more than one child at a time.

# 2. Elevated Sand-Tables

24" reach

32" ht. max.

sand

■ elevated area containing sand or water provides access for those in wheelchairs. Flat area is useful for toy cars, crafts, etc.

# 3. Basketball Hoops

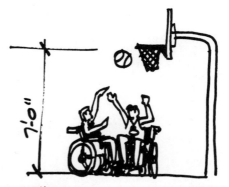

7'-0"

■ basketball hoops lowered to 7'-0" from standard 10'-0" ht. allow those in wheelchairs and young children to enjoy the game.

adult supervision. The amount of supervision varies depending on the type of handicap the child has, the type of equipment present, and the number of handicapped children using the facility. This may mean that in certain cases, parents will have to accompany their child in order that they may supervise his play. In other cases, a single attendant may be sufficient.

6. A series of small vignettes have been prepared to illustrate some of the many recreational devices that can be incorporated into play grounds and can be used by most handicapped children.

Further information about publications on recreational facilities, facility designs and locations of specific recreational facilities, is listed in the bibliography in the back of this report.

# Camping, Cooking and Picnicking

For a camping facility to provide a good range of experiences for nearly everyone, it should generally include the following items:

- Level terrain around high-use areas such as shelters, lavatories, swimming pools or beaches, food preparation areas, etc.
- Swimming facilities.
- Adequate acreage to promote the "camping experience" and buffer zones to instill a sense of remoteness.
- Good recreation potential with prime consideration given to water-based activities.
- Ease of access and good communications.
- Good medical facilities close at hand.

1. **Campsites:**
   a. Dangerous obstructions should be removed from the general campsite area. Tree branches should be pruned above 8'-6" off the ground.

   b. Water faucets and comfort facilities should be located no more than 100' to 200' from campsites.

   c. Access to all areas in the campsite should

be over hard surface paths.

d. Eating and service tables should be set on a hard surface so that they are accessible to everyone.

e. For group camping units, the kitchen area and sleeping areas should be separated from each other, both for reasons of functional segregation and to minimize the impact of the two areas upon the site.

f. Each group unit should have its own water faucet and disposal facilities.

2. **Cooking:**
   a. **Fireplaces:**
      1. A fireplace that is raised 18" to 24" off the ground is easier to use from a seated position than a ground level fireplace.

   b. **Grills:**
      1. For cooking food over charcoal, a grill is more convenient than a fireplace.
      2. The clearance from the ground to the top of the unit should be a maximum of 30".
      3. Grills should rotate 360°, to allow a person seated in a wheelchair the ability to reach all parts of the grill without having to move.
      4. Grills should be protected by asbestos sheeting placed 1" away from the exterior walls.
      5. Grills should have wings upon which to set utensils.
      6. Grills should be placed where there is hard-surface access.

   c. **Water faucets:**
      1. Water faucets located at a 3'-4" height are easily operable by most people.
      2. They should preferably be actuated by a lever rather than by a standard gate valve since levers are easier to operate for the majority of people. If a gate valve is used, it should not have a spring return mechanism. These devices increase the difficulty in opening the valve.
      3. They should be accessible over a hard surface.
      4. A drain should be used to carry away the

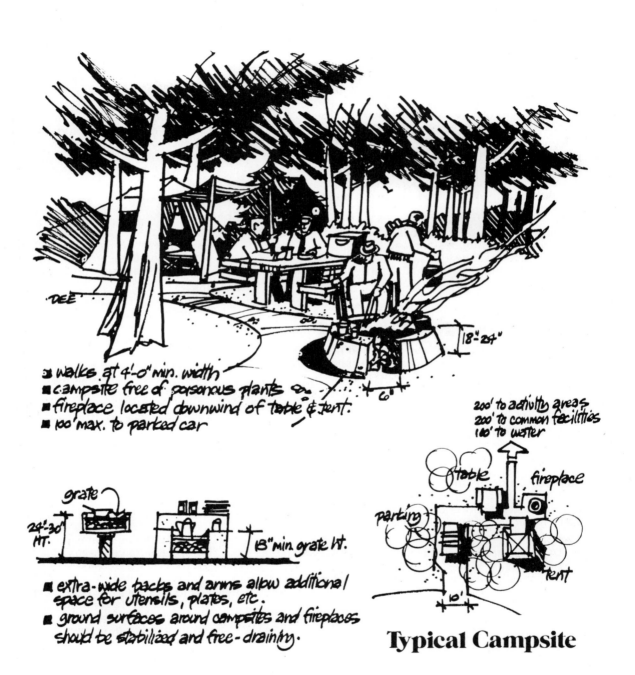

- walks at 4'-0" min. width
- campsite free of poisonous plants
- fireplace located downwind of table & tent
- 100' max. to parked car

DEE

18"-24"

6'

grate

24"-30" HT.

18" min. grate ht.

- extra-wide backs and arms allow additional space for utensils, plates, etc.
- ground surfaces around campsites and fireplaces should be stabilized and free-draining.

200' to activity areas
200' to common facilities
100' to water

table
fireplace
parking
tent
10'

**Typical Campsite**

# Interpretive Trails for the Handicapped

■ SIGNS SHOULD IDENTIFY FACTS ABOUT AREA. CONFORM TO RECOMMENDATIONS IN SECTION ON <u>SIGNAGE.</u>

■ PROVIDE RAILINGS OR ROPE ALONG EDGE TO HELP DEFINE TRAIL OR TO WARN OF DANGER AREAS.

3'-0" min. width
4'-0" preferred

■ CHANGE OF TEXTURE HELPS TO IDENTIFY SIGN OR REST AREA. PAVING SHOULD BE FIRM AND FREE-DRAINING.

■ PRECAST CURBS HELP TO DEFINE EDGE OF TRAIL.

overflow either into a drainage system or into a gravel drain.

3. **Picnicking:**

Picnicking is a recreational pastime that is enjoyed by all types of people. With a few alterations, existing picnicking facilities can be used by a greater diversity of people.

The following factors should be considered in the design of picnic facilities:

a. Good access to the site over a hard surface which is free of obstructions.

b. A comfort station and drinking fountain located within 100' to 200' from the picnic area.

c. Level surfaced areas around some picnic tables designed to accommodate wheelchair dependent people.

d. Raised fireplaces.

e. Grills.

f. A picnic shelter area.

g. Picnic tables should be placed on a hard surface at least 3" to 4" wider on each side than the table since certain people such as mothers with strollers, people on crutches, or chair-bound people are unable to negotiate softer surfaces with ease.

h. A 29" minimum of space should be allowed between the bottom edge of the table and the ground to allow a wheelchair to slide under the table.

i. See "Lighting Considerations."

# Interpretive Trails

Interpretive trails should be designed to allow for the greatest diversity of people to use them. As such, they will need to be well organized and detailed. The main purpose of interpretive trails is to please and inform.

The following items should be taken into consideration in the design of interpretive trails:

1. There should be a sign at the beginning of the trail in braille and raised or routed letters that gives information on the following items:

a. How long the trail is.

b. The locations of special areas such as rest stops and comfort facilities.

c. The location and height of signs in braille and raised or routed letters (that accommodate both the blind and the sighted population) describing events along the trail and calling out particularly interesting items to view or touch.

d. The meaning of special signals such as textural changes in the walks.

e. Any dangerous areas.

2. **Signs to Assist the Blind:**

a. A 3'-0" high rope line used along at least one side of a trail, and along both sides where the trail curves sharply, is a useful guide to blind people.

b. Knots tied in the rope prior to rest-stops, comfort stations and trail stops let the person know tactilely of their location.

c. Pre-recorded messages may be heard either by pushing a button which activates the recording, or by the use of a continuously worn headset which receives the transmitted message as it comes into range.

3. The trail surface should be firm and clear of debris or obstructions. Materials such as soil cement, compacted trap rock dust, or asphalt are suitable for light or moderate traffic.

# Spectator Areas

Spectator areas should be provided in locations adjacent to sports functions to allow for at least a minimal side-line participation in sporting events. The same requirements also apply to other spectator areas such as indoor and outdoor theaters.

# Amphitheaters

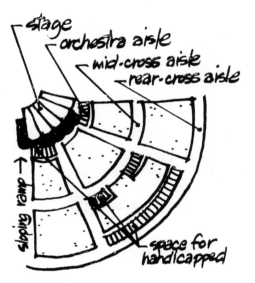

stage
orchestra aisle
mid-cross aisle
rear-cross aisle

sloping bridges

space for handicapped

■ provide spaces for handicapped and wheelchairs at all levels of amphitheater, accessable by ramp.
■ seats should allow extra space for extended leg braces.

The following factors should be considered in the design of spectator facilities:

1. Spectator areas should be spread out to allow a choice in seating areas.

2. Where possible, these seats should have protection from the sun, rain, and wind, but this protection should not diminish vision of the playing area.

3. Spectator areas should have a firm surface with good access.

4. Ramps as well as stairs should be provided.

5. Properly designed areas for wheelchairs.

6. In seating areas with an excess of 75 seats, a minimum of 1 seat or 2% of the total seating (whichever is greater) should be allotted for wheelchairs. Likewise, 1 seat or 1% of the total seating should be designed to accommodate people on crutches or people using walkers.

## Boating-Fishing

1. Boating may be enjoyed by many physically handicapped people, provided that a few adaptations are made to accommodate them. The problems are primarily, (1) access to the boat, and (2) the inclusion of supportive devices within the boat itself.

Specifically, the following factors should be considered:

a. Access to the docks should be over hard surfaces, free of clutter, and devoid of situations which might prove hazardous for the person with a physical limitation.

b. Docks should have handrails and railings 3'-0" high, designed in such a way as to allow a person to support himself while he travels along the dock, as well as while he enters the boat.

105

■ provide 5 footcandle lighting in ramp and dock areas.

■ provide ramp with minimum 32" clear opening width and maximum gradient 10%.

■ access to dock area should be across firm paving surface suitable for wheelchair.

■ provide life ring and ladders for use in emergency.

**Waterfront Areas**

■ provide secure handrails for support in walking and to prevent objects or people from falling into water.

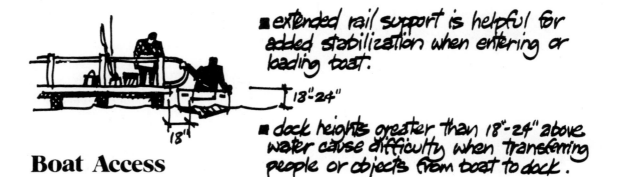

■ extended rail support is helpful for added stabilization when entering or loading boat.

18"-24"

**Boat Access**

18"

■ dock heights greater than 18"-24" above water cause difficulty when transferring people or objects from boat to dock.

c. Entry of the boat from the dock should always be from a position perpendicular or parallel to the dock. These two positions allow for the safest entry into a boat.

d. Once within the boat, hand grasps or rails should be provided to assist a person in moving about. This pertains mostly to larger boats, as the addition of such equipment could present more potential hazards than benefits in a small boat or canoe.

2. Fishing is an extremely popular activity for all types of people, and one that is relatively easy to accommodate since all that is really necessary is to provide access to the water.

One should consider the following factors when designing fishing facilities:

a. Hard-surfaced access to and along the water's edge.

b. Access out over the water through one of the following means:
   .1. A stable fishing pier that extends far enough out over the water to account for both high and low water lines.
   2. A floating fishing pier built long enough to account for both high and low water lines.

c. Piers should be equipped with railings designed with shelves to accommodate fishing paraphernalia.

# Swimming

Swimming has long been considered a popular sport as well as being recognized for its therapeutic value to the handicapped. If a swimming facility is to be designed for therapeutic use in addition to accommodating the general public, a pool is preferred over lake facilities because of better control over water depth, temperature, supervision and sanitation.

1. **Swimming Pools:**
   a. Accessibility to swimming pools designed to accommodate a diversity of people can be provided in two ways:
      1. At various locations, the pool coping can be raised above the pool deck 1'-7" and fitted with grab bars that allow people who have difficulty crouching, or who are wheelchair dependent, to first sit and then swing their legs over the side into the water.
      2. The pool coping can be made level with the water with just enough slope to drain off any water splashed from the pool.

   b. Along with both of the above types of pool copings, there should be a ramp with handrails, and a set of stairs with handrails, both located at the shallow end of the pool.

   c. Pools having more shallow area than is usual are preferred by many people who enjoy the security of knowing they can touch bottom at any time. If diving is a requirement, then an additional pool should be considered.

2. **Lake Swimming:**
   The major disadvantages to lake swimming arise for the most part in regard to people who are handicapped, because of lack of control over water depth, temperature, supervision, and sanitation control.

   The designer should consider the following items when attempting to make a swimming area accessible to the handicapped:

   a. Preferably, the grade of the beach into the water should be no more than 10%.

   b. An access walk leading to and along the water's edge is necessary.

   c. A ramp with handrail along one side extending into the water to a depth of 3'-0" should be provided.

   d. The entire swimming area should be well marked with floating markers or signals.

■ space for wheelchair-bound spectators located near entrance ramp minimizes need to maneuver through crowd. Access aisle should be _behind_ handicapped spectators.

■ access to viewing stands from parking should be on firm surface suitable for wheelchairs.

■ provide each wheelchair space @ 30" wide.

■ access ramp min. 4'-0" width, preferred 6'-0". Maximum gradient recommended 10%.

4'-0" typical

4'-0" minimum clear aisle    3'-6" minimum

7'-6" min. - 8'-0" preferred

# Section Through Spectator Stands

# Considerations for Pool Swimming

■ Provide stairs whenever possible rather than a ladder. Stairs are more easily negotiated and can be used to sit upon if wide enough.

■ Floats and pavement markings should clearly warn swimmers of increasing depth of water.

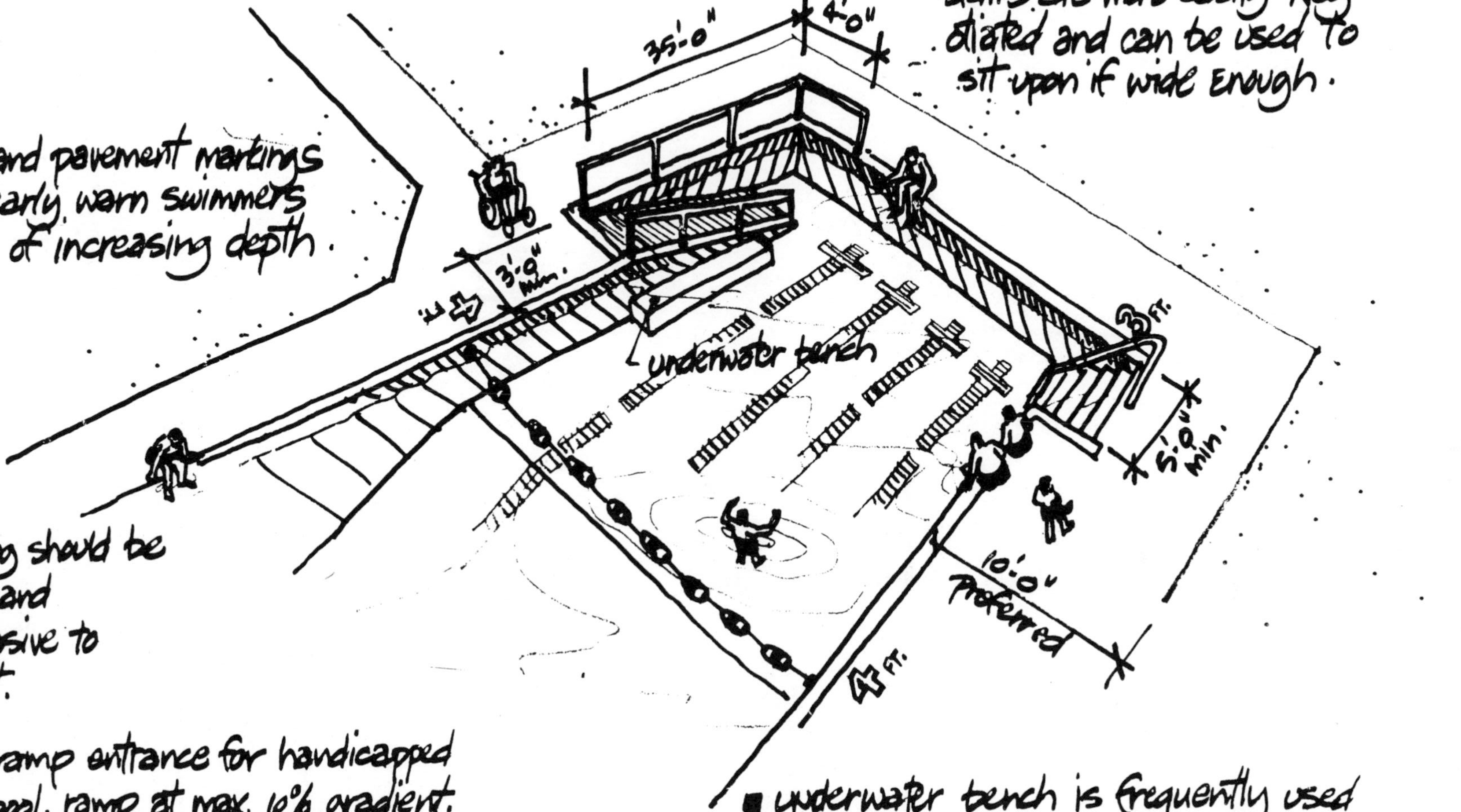

■ All paving should be non-slip and non-abrasive to bare feet.

■ Provide ramp entrance for handicapped to enter pool. Ramp at max. 10% gradient. Surface should be non-slip and have curb at edge. Handrails provided on both sides at 36" height.

■ Underwater bench is frequently used by handicapped for resting. Location should prohibit other swimmers from jumping from above. Use rounded edges throughout.

5'-0" min.

10'-0" preferred

4'-0"

35'-0"

3'-0" min.

sand beach

109

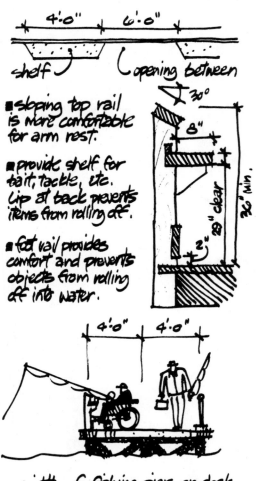

- sloping top rail is more comfortable for arm rest.

- provide shelf for bait, tackle, etc. Lip at back prevents items from rolling off.

- fat rail provides comfort and prevents objects from rolling off into water.

- width of fishing pier or dock should allow free movement of pedestrians when wheelchair is perpendicular to edge.

# Fishing Docks & Piers

e. Because of the difficulties in regulating a lake swimming facility, the addition of a swimming pool should be considered, especially if the lake is also used extensively for boating, fishing, skiing, and other water functions.

## Considerations for Lake Swimming

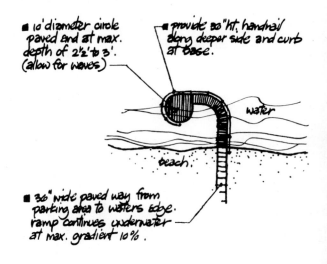

- 10' diameter circle paved and at max. depth of 2'2" to 3'. (allow for waves)

- provide 30" ht. handrail along deeper side and curb at base.

- 36" wide paved way from parking area to waters edge. ramp continues underwater at max. gradient 10%.

NOTE: length of ramped walk should be adjusted to slope of particular lake profile, (10% max. gradient.) and should consider size of anticipated waves.

110

# Site Furniture

## Outdoor Tables

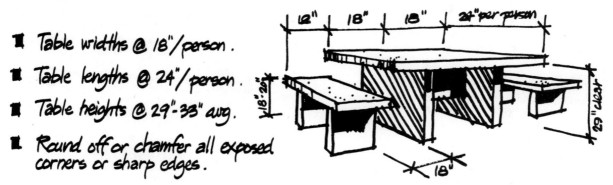

- Table widths @ 18"/person.

- Table lengths @ 24"/person.

- Table heights @ 29"-33" avg.

- Round off or chamfer all exposed corners or sharp edges.

- Keep table tops smooth with no recesses that might hold water or food particles.

- Provide 18" clear leg space under table; measure from outside of table top to nearest support or table leg, etc.

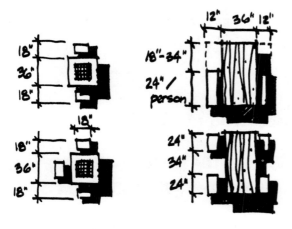

**Game Tables**     **Picnic Tables**

The following data represents design recommendations in regard to the most commonly used elements of site furniture. The criteria shown are intended to enhance the use of specific types of furniture by a greater diversity of people.

1. **Tables:**
   **a.** Tables should be constructed with a clear space between the ground and bottom edge of the table of at least 29". This allows wheelchair dependent people to pull up beneath the tabletop.

   **b.** A lateral space of at least 34" is necessary to account for the width of a wheelchair.

   **c.** At least some tables intended for public use should be located on hard surface paved areas. Mothers with children in strollers or carriages, people who are physically restricted in their movements, and wheelchair dependent people are better able to gain access to these tables.

2. **Seating:**
   **a.** Seating should be provided adjacent to paved areas, along walks, near the tops and bottoms of major ramps and stairs, and where otherwise deemed appropriate. It should not be located within a traveled way where it would create an obstruction.

   **b.** Seat heights in a given area should be uniform and at a height from the ground of 18" to 20".

   **c.** Seats should be designed with back supports and arm rests. Aside from being desirable from a standpoint of comfort, they also provide support for people rising up off the seat.

   **d.** Seating should be constructed to support a minimum of 250 lbs. for each person they are designed to accommodate.

   **e.** A space of 5'-0" should be allowed between the front of a seat and the nearest obstacle. A space 36" wide between ends of benches, or at the end of one bench, allows

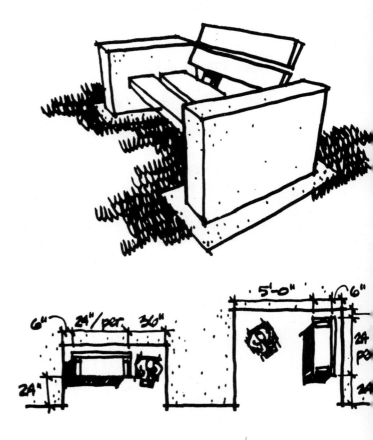

## Space Around a Bench

■ PROVIDE 24" SETBACK TO KEEP LEGS FROM INTERRUPTING ADJACENT PEDESTRIAN TRAFFIC

■ A 36" MIN. SPACE SHOULD BE PROVIDED TO ALLOW ROOM FOR WHEELCHAIRS.

# Benches & Outdoor Seating

- CHOOSE MATERIALS WHICH DO NOT RETAIN HEAT OR COLD. AVOID ROUGH MATERIALS OR THOSE THAT MAY SPLINTER.

- SITTING HEIGHTS OF 18"-20" ARE PREFERABLE.

- SITTING SURFACES BELOW 12" WIDTH ARE UNCOMFORTABLE FOR MANY ADULTS. LIKEWISE, WIDTHS BEYOND 18" BECOME AWKWARD FOR NORMAL LEG LENGTHS.

- PROVISIONS FOR ARM AND BACK RESTS INCREASE COMFORT. ARM RESTS ARE ALSO HELPFUL FOR GETTING INTO AND OUT OF SEATS AND BENCHES.

- PROVISION FOR HEEL SPACE OF 3" MAKES RISING FROM SEATED POSITION EASIER.

- SEAT SURFACES SHOULD BE PITCHED TO SHED WATER.

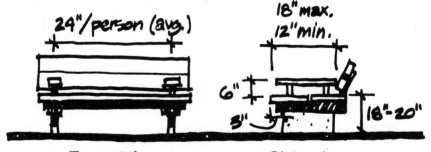

24"/person (avg.)

18" max.
12" min.

6"

3"

18"-20"

**Front View**          **Side View**

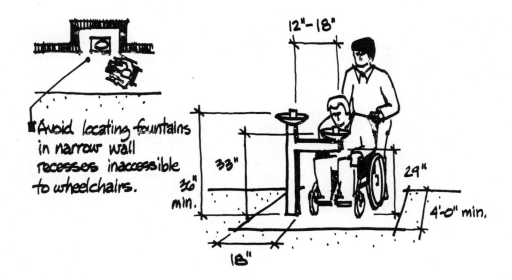

Avoid locating fountains in narrow wall recesses inaccessible to wheelchairs.

# Drinking Fountains

▪ Hand operated knobs or buttons and foot pedals are difficult for many handicapped people to operate. Hand levers are preferred.

▪ Provide a minimum 29" vertical clearance below fountain nozzle to allow wheelchairs leg room for access.

▪ Nozzle heights should be approximately 33" for wheelchairs and children and 36" to 39" for adults.

▪ A minimum 18" wide paved area around outdoor fountains avoids both mud and puddles.

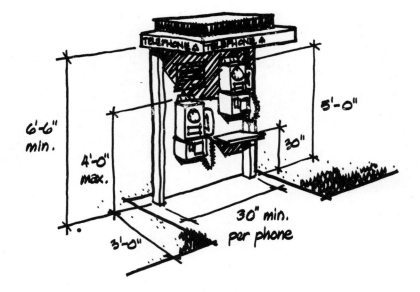

## Outdoor Telephones

■ All groups of telephones should have at least one lower height telephone for use by the handicapped and children.

■ Phones for the handicapped should be no higher than 4'-0" at the coin slots. Provisions for braille instructions, volume controls on headsets, and push button dials are helpful for many handicapped individuals.

■ Provide adequate lighting on the underside of overhangs for nighttime use.

■ Package rests are a helpful convenience to all people.

room for strollers and wheelchairs to park.

3. **Telephones:**

All installations of outdoor telephones should include at least one unit that is usable by people not able to use standard telephones. To this end, the following items should be considered:

**a.** Access to the unit should be over a hard surface.

**b.** The installation should be located either entirely out of doors or, if enclosed, should be spacious enough to permit access by a wheelchair.

**c.** The top of the telephone should be no higher than 4'-0" above the floor.

**d.** Public telephones should be operable by push buttons.

**e.** Telephone books should be located approximately 30" above the floor.

**f.** A fold-up seat should be provided at a height between 18" and 20".

**g.** A volume control should be provided in an out-of-the-way place on the telephone to aid the hard-of-hearing.

**h.** Consult with phone company for their standards and details offered concerning the needs of handicapped individuals.

**i.** Design of surrounding facilities (doorways, openings, hallways, etc.) should comply with operational requirements as outlined in "Basic Human Considerations" section.

4. **Switches, Buttons, Sockets and Wall-Mounted Appurtenances:**

Switches for lights, buttons for elevators and street crossings, electrical sockets, fire extinguishers, alarm boxes, etc., should be placed no higher than 4'-0" from the floor. Pull down levers or control knobs of any kind should not require more than 8 lbs. of force to operate them.

5. **Drinking Fountains**

In order that a greater diversity of people from small children to wheelchair dependent individuals may be accommodated by drinking fountains, the following items should be considered:

**a.** In all areas, fountains should be placed on hard surface areas or immediately adjacent to hard surfaces in order to be accessible to wheelchair dependent people.

**b.** It may be necessary to design a free-standing unit that has two fountains; one for normal ambulant adults, and a lower fountain for children and wheelchair dependent people.

**c.** Fully recessed fountains should be avoided unless adequate space is allotted for wheelchair access.

**d.** Controls for drinking fountains should be hand-operated levers rather than knobs. Spring-loaded return mechanisms should not be used in conjunction with either levers or knobs since the force required to activate these devices is more than some people are able to exert. Both the lever and the bubbler should be located at the front of the fountain.

**e.** Stepping blocks, often provided to enable children to reach the bubbler, should be located so as not to interfere with access to the fountain either by totally ambulant people or wheelchair dependent people.

6. **Trash Receptacles**

**a.** Trash receptacles should be of a type that may be operated by a single hand movement.

**b.** The opening of a trash receptacle should be approximately 3'-0" above the ground. Spring-loaded doors or doors that are foot-operated should not be used.

**c.** The receptacle should be strong enough to provide support for people who may require it in order to use the receptacle.

**d.** Edges should be crimped, rounded, or smoothed to prevent cuts or abrasions.

# Trash Cans & Receptacles

3'-0" max. to opening

**1.** Open top easiest to discard trash; open to rain, wind, snow; needs weep holes for drainage; easy to empty; open to insects.

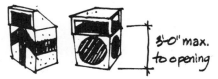

3'-0" max. to opening

**2.** Semi-open top gives protection from elements; top hinged to allow removal of trash when unit is full; openings must be designed to accept size of anticipated trash; open to insects.

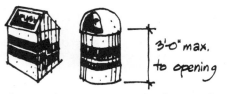

3'-0" max. to opening

**3.** Hinged-door openings are difficult for many handicapped people to operate; good protection from elements and insects; openings must be designed for anticipated trash sizes; spring loaded doors should be easily pushed open with one hand.

120

# Bibliography

The following is a very selected listing of reference materials pertinent to physical design (especially site design) to allow full access to the environment. This is by no means all of the available reference material.  More is being developed, updated, or outdated each day, and it would take a very sophisticated computer system and program to have a fully current listing at any given time.  There are some especially important or pertinent documents; these are listed, as are major bibliographices which catalog many of the other most relevant documents. This is not meant to be a definitive bibliography; it is an appropriate beginning in your search for more data.

*A Brief Checklist of Recent Publications Relating to Architectural Planning for the Physically Handicapped,* The National Easter Seal Society for Crippled Children and Adults, 2023 West Ogden Ave., Chicago, Ill. 60612.

*Access Chicago: Architects' and Designers Handbook of Barrier-Free Design,* The Rehabilitation Institute of Chicago, Chicago, Ill. 1974.

*Accessibility Modifications, Guidelines for Modification to Existing Buildings for Accessibility to the Handicapped,* North Carolina Department of Insurance, Engineering and Buildng Codes Division, Raleigh, North Carolina 27611, 63 pp.

*Accessibility Standards Illustrated,* Michael A. Jones, Illinois Capital Development Board, Third Floor, William G. Stratton Building, 401 South Spring Street, Springfield, Ill. 62706, 1978, 217 pp.

*Access to the Environment* (3 volumes) Developed by the American Society of Landscape Architects Foundation, (Edited by Gary O. Robinette), available from the Office of Policy Development and Research, Department of Housing and Urban Development, HUD User, P.O. Box 280, Germantown, Maryland 20767, 1978.

Access Resources Lists:
    *Playgrounds*
    *Recreation*
    *Environments for All Children*
Available from the:
    National Center for a Barrier-Free Environment
    1140 Connecticut Ave., N.W., Suite 1006
    Washington, D.C. 20036

*Accessibility: the Law and the Reality, A Survey to Test the Application and Effectiveness of Public Law 90-480 in Iowa,* Iowa Chapter, American Institute of Architects, 621 Savings & Loan Building, Des Moines, Iowa 50309.

*Access for All: An Illustrated Handbook of Barrier-Free Design for Ohio,* Robert D. Loversidge, Jr., editor, Ohio Governor's Committe on Employment of the Handicapped, 4656 Heaton Road, Columbus, Ohio 43229, 1979, 190 pp.

*Access to Play, Design Criteria for Adaptation of Existing Playground Equipment for Use by Handicapped Children,* Pittsburgh Architect's Workshop, 237 Oakland Ave., Pittsburgh, PA. 15213, 1979, 102 pp.

*Access to Recreation, Design Criteria for Eliminating Architectural Barriers,* Indiana Department of Natural Resources, Division of Outdoor Recreation, 612 State Office Building, Indianapolis, Indiana, 1981, 56 pp.

*A Guide to Designing Accessible Outdoor Recreation Facilities,* Heritage Conservation and Recreation Service, U.S. Department of the Interior, Lake Central Region, Ann Arbor, Michigan 48107, 1980, 58 pp.

*ANSI A117.1(1980) Specifications for Making Buildings and Facilities Accessible to and Usable by Physically Handicapped People,* American National Standards Institute, Inc., 1430 Broadway, New York, N.Y. 10018.

*An Illustrated Handbook of the Handicapped Section of the North Carolina State Building Code,* Ronald L. Mace and Betsy Laslett, editors, available from the North Carolina Department of Insurance, Engineering Division, P.O. Box 26387, Raleigh, North Carolina 27611, 1977, 122 pp.

*Architectural Accessibility for the Disabled on College Campuses,* Stephen R. Cotler and Alfred H. DeGraff, New York State University Construction Fund, 194 Washington Ave., Albany, N.Y. 12210, 1976.

*A Playground for All Children: Book 3 Resource Book,* Mona Levine and Saul Nimowitz, available from the Superintendent of Documents, U.S. Government Printing Office, Washington, D.C., 1978, 62 pp.

*Architectural Barriers:Bibliography,* Reference Services, Library of Congress/Division of the Blind and Physically Handicapped, Washington, D.C. 20542.

*Barrier-Free Design,* Susan Hammerman and Barbara Duncan(editors), Rehabilitation International, New York, N.Y., 1975.

*Barrier-Free Design - Accessibility for the Handicapped,* Phyllis L. Tica and Julius A. Shaw, Institute for Research and Development in Occupational Education, Publication No. Case-06-74, 1976, 31 pp.

*Barrier-Free Design: A Selected Bibliography,* Peter Lassen, distributed by the Michigan Paralyzed Veterans of America, 30406 Ford Road, Garden City, Michigan 48135.

*Barrier-Free Site Design,* Developed by the American Society of Landscape Architects Foundation for the Office of Policy Development and Research, U.S. Department of Housing and Urban Development, available from the Superintendent of Documents, U.S. Government Printing Office, Washington, D.C. 20402, Stock Number 023-000-00291-4, 1975, 82 pp.

*The BOCA Basic Building Code, 1975; 6th Edition,* Building Officials and Code Administrators International, Inc., Danville, Ill., 1975.

*CFR Part 1190, Minimum Guidelines and Requirements for Accessible Design,* Architectural and Transportation Barriers Compliance Board, Federal Register, January 16, 1981, 33 pp.

*Day on Wheels,* Public Building Service, General Services Administration, Washington, D.C., January 1975, 120 pp.

*Design Criteria - New Public Building Accessibility,* Public Building Service, General Services Administration, PBS (PCD): DG5, Washington, D.C., May 1977, 157 pp.

*Design for Access,* N.M. Spencer, California Paralyzed Veterans Association, Huntington Beach, CA., 1976.

*Design Standards to Accommodate People with Physical Disabilities in Park and Open Space Planning,* Michael L. Ries, available from the Recreation Resource Center, University of Wisconsin-Extension, 1815 University Avenue, Madison, Wisconsin 53706, 1973, 74 pp.

*Designing for the Disabled,* Selwin Goldsmith, McGraw-Hill Book Co., New York, N.Y., 1967, 207 pp.

*Building Without Barriers for the Disabled,* Sarah P. Harkness and James N. Groom,Jr., Whitney Library of Design, Watson-Guptill Publishing Co., New York, 1978, 79 pp.

*Assessing Physical Barriers in a University Setting,* Robert M. Harris, A. Christine Harris and Donald Whipple, Department of Psychology and Architectural Services, University of Kansas, Lawrence, Kansas.

*Annotated Bibliography on Building for Disabled Persons,* Division of Building Research, National Research Council, Ottawa, Canada, 1971.

*Humanscale 1/2/3,* Neils, Diffrient, M.I.T. Press, Cambridge, MA., 1974.

*The Measure of Man: Human Factors in Design,* Henry Dreyfuss, Whitney Library of Design, Watson-Guptill Publishing Co., New York, N.Y., 1967.

*Housing and Handicapped People,* Marie McGuire Thompson, President's Committee on Employment of the Handicapped, Washington, D.C., 1976.

*Housing for the Handicapped and Disabled: A Guide for Local Action,* National Association of Housing and Redevelopment Officials, 2600 Virginia Ave., N.W., Washington, D.C. 20037, 1977, 176 pp.

*Housing for the Handicapped and Disabled: A Guide for Local Action,* Marie McGuire Thompson, National Association of Housing and Redevelopment Officials, 2600 Virginia Avenue, N.W., Washington, D.C. 20037, 1977, 176 pp.

*Housing the Handicapped,* Central Mortgage and Housing Corporation, NHA 5076, Ottawa, Canada, 1974, 120 pp.

*Into the Mainstream: A Syllabus for a Barrier-Free Environment,* S.A. Kliment, available from the American Institute of Architects, Publications Manager, 1735 New York Ave.,N.W., Washington, D.C. 20006, 1975, 44 pp.

*Interpretation for Handicapped Persons, A Handbook for Outdoor Recreation Personnel,* Jacque Beechel, National Park Service, Pacific Northwest Region, Cooperative Park Studies Unit, College of Forest Resources, University of Washington, Seattle, WA. 98195, 59 pp.

*Mainstreaming Handicapped Individuals: Parks and Recreation Design Standards Manual,* Dr. Silas P. Singh, available from Handicapped Program Coordinator, Illinois Department of Conservation, 605 State Office Building, Springfield, Illinois 62706, 1978, 48 pp.

*Making Physical Education and Recreation Facilities Accessible to All,* American Alliance for Health, Physical Education, Recreation and Dance, availabel from AAHPERD Publications, P.O. Box 704, 44 Industrial Park Circle, Waldorf, Maryland 20601, 1977, 138 pp.

*Mobile Homes: Alternative Housing for the Handicapped.,* Ronald L. Mace, U.S. Department of Housing and Urban Development, 1977, 48 pp.

*Modifications of New York State Parks for Disabled Individuals, Section I - Recommendations; Section II - Bibliography,* Linda Nierenberg and Michael Berthold, available from the Human Resources Center, I.U. Willets Road, Albertson, New York, N.Y. 11507, 1977, 57 pp.

*Outdoor Recreation for the Physically Handicapped,* available from the Indiana Department of Natural Resources, Division of Outdoor Recreation, 612 State Office Building, Indianapolis, Indiana 46204, 1978, 47 pp.

*Outdoor Recreation for the Mentally Ill, Mentally Retarded, Physically Disabled and Aging in Illinois: A Five Year Plan,* Carol Peterson, available from the University of Illinois, Office of Recreation and Park Resources, Department of Leisure Studies, 312 Armory Building, Champaign, Illinois 61820, 1977, 345 pp.

*Planning for Accessibility: A Guide to Developing and Implementing Campus Transition Plans,* Margaret Milner, American Association of Physical Plant Administrators of Universities and Colleges, Eleven Dupont Circle, Suite 250, Washington, D.C. 20036, 1978, 88 pp.

*Publications Available from the National Easter Seal Society for Crippled Children and Adults,* available from the NESCCA, 2023 West Ogden Ave., Chicago, Ill. 60612.

*Resource Guide to Literature on Barrier-Free Environments,* Architectural and Transportation Barriers Compliance Board, U.S. Department of Health, Education and Welfare, Washington, D.C. 1977.

*Technical Handbook for Facilities Engineering and Construction - Manual Part 4 - Facilities Design and Construction, 4.00 Architectural Section 4.12: Design of Barrier Free Facilities,* Office of Architectural and Engineering Services, OFEPM/DHEW, 330 Independence Ave., S.W., Washington, D.C. 20201.

*Tools for Accessibility, A Selected List of Resources for Barrier-Free Design,* National Center for a Barrier-Free Environment, Suite 1006, 1140 Connecticut Ave., N.W., Washington, D.C. 20036, 1981, 12 pp.

*Urban Wheelchair Use: A Human Factors Analysis,* Peter Wachter, Rehabilitation Institute of Chicago, Chicago, Ill., 1976.

The following publications were prepared by the staff at the Syracuse University, School of Architecture under contract with the Office of Policy Development and Research of the U.S. Department of Housing and Urban Development and are available from the Superintendent of Documents, U.S. Government Printing Office, Washington, D.C. 20402.

> *Selected Bibliography on Barrier-Free Design*
> *Access to the Built Environment: A Review of Literature*
> *An Outline of Provision for a Uniform Barrier-Free Design Act*
> *Adaptable Dwellings*
> *A Cost-Benefit Analysis of Accessibility*
> *Accessible Buildings for People with Walking and Reaching Limitations*
> *The Estimated Cost of Accessible Buildings*
> *Accessible Buildings for People with Severe Visual Limitations.*